Revising the Eucharist: Groundwork for the Anglican Communion

Studies in preparation for the 1995 Dublin Consultation

edited by David R. Holeton

Dean of Trinity College, Toronto
Chair of the International Anglican Liturgical Consultation

Copyright David R. Holeton

THE ALCUIN CLUB and the GROUP FOR RENEWAL OF WORSHIP (GROW)

The Alcuin Club, which exists to promote the study of Christian liturgy in general and of Anglican liturgy in particular, traditionally published a single volume annually for its members. This ceased in 1986 but resumed in 1992. Similarly, GROW was responsible from 1975 to 1986 for the quarterly 'Grove Liturgical Studies'. Since the beginning of 1987 the two have sponsored a Joint Editorial Board to produce quarterly 'Joint Liturgical Studies', details of which are to be found at the end of this Study.

THE COVER PICTURE

is a reproduction of the very distincive alternative form of blessing in the 1989 modern eucharistic rite of the Church of the Province of Kenya

First Impression March 1994
ISSN 0951-2667
ISBN 1 85174 262 X

GROVE BOOKS LIMITED
Bramcote   Nottingham   NG9 3DS

CONTENTS

THE CONTRIBUTORS

Paul Bradshaw is Professor of Liturgy at the University of Notre Dame and President of Societas Liturgica.

Colin Buchanan is Vicar of St. Mark's Gillingham and Honorary Assistant Bishop of Rochester in the Church of England.

William Crockett is Professor of Systematic Theology at the Vancouver School of Theology.

Ronald Dowling is Rector of the Church of St. Mary the Virgin, South Perth, Australia.

John Gibaut is Assistant Professor in the Faculty of Theology at St. Paul University, Ottawa.

Paul Gibson is Liturgical Officer of the Anglican Church of Canada.

David Holeton is Dean of Divinity at Trinity College, Toronto and Chair of the International Anglican Liturgical Consultation.

David Kennedy is Chaplain at The Queen's College, Birmingham.

Gillian Mendham is Chaplain to the Australian National University, a member of the Australian Anglican Liturgical Commission and Editor of A Prayer Book for Australia 1995.

Ruth Meyers is Diocesan Liturgist in the Diocese of Western Michigan and Associate Faculty Member of the Ecumenical Theological Center, Detroit.

Harold Miller is Rector of Carrigrohane, Co. Cork in the Church of Ireland.

Clayton Morris is the Programme Coordinator for Liturgy and Music of the Episcopal Church, USA.

Juan Quevedo-Bosch is Professor of Liturgy at the Seminario Evangelico de Theologia, Matanzas, Cuba.

Charles Sherlock is Professor of Theology at Ridley College, Parkville, Melbourne, Australia.

David Smart is a doctoral student in liturgy and church architecture at Trinity College, Toronto.

Bryan Spinks is Chaplain to the Chapel at Churchill College, Cambridge and a member of the Church of England Liturgical Commission.

Kenneth Stevenson is Rector of Holy Trinity and St. Mary's Guildford and a member of the Church of England Liturgical Commission.

Thomas Talley is Professor Emeritus of Liturgy at the General Theological Seminary, New York

Phillip Tovey is Team Vicar of Banbury in the Diocese of Oxford.

Charles Wallace is a theological student at Trinity College, Toronto, and was administrator of the Untermarchtal Conference.

Introduction

by the Editor David R. Holeton

At its Fourth Consultation in Toronto, the International Anglican Liturgical Consultation identified the eucharist as a topic that needed to be addressed in the same way as Christian initiation had been at IALC-4. The widespread attention and favourable reaction received by the Toronto Statement *Walk in Newness of Life* encouraged the Steering Committee in this resolve.

When the Steering Committee met in Winchester in July 1992 to begin its planning for the next Consultation, which was scheduled to be held in August 1993, the realities of the present economic recession hit home. Most of the representatives of less economically developed provinces and member churches who were present at IALC-4 had been assisted through the generosity of two provinces. It was made clear that this financial support would not be available on a biennial basis.

Instead of calling a full Consultation, the Steering Committee decided to go ahead with a Conference of the IALC for which no financial assistance would be made available. While the Steering Committee was aware of the effect this decision would have on the representative nature of the Conference, it was also acknowledged that the breadth and complexity of the issues involved in the subject required a preliminary meeting at which some of these issues would be delineated. This became the primary purpose of the 1993 Conference which was held at the Bildungshaus in Untermarchtal, Swabia, Germany.

Professor Thomas Talley and Bishop Colin Buchanan were asked to present papers which would outline as they saw them the major issues which would face those engaged in eucharistic reform and renewal over the coming years. These papers are printed first in this volume. The Conference members were divided into four working groups which addressed the broad areas of (1) eucharistic theology, (2) ritual, language and symbolism of the eucharist, (3) structure of the eucharistic rite and (4) ministry, order and the eucharist. The short essays printed after the two main papers in this volume try to sketch out some of the issues that were raised in the context of those discussions.

The reader will quickly recognize that the issues are diverse and touch on issues that often come very close to the heart. The essays were written in the hope of precipitating widespread discussion before IALC-5 is held in Dublin in August 1995. They should be regarded as preparatory and not as a final word in the debate that is yet to take place. The issues they raise will appear on the agenda of IALC-5 and will likely find a place in the Dublin Statement. This volume is intended to inform and not preclude that debate.

Once again, IALC is indebted to Alcuin/GROW for making the circulation of this material throughout the Communion possible. I am also particularly grateful to David Smart whose help as assistant editor made the welding of the wide variety of submissions into a single volume possible.

1. Eucharistic Prayers, Past, Present and Future

by Thomas Talley

Let me begin with a couple of disclaimers. First, while there is much more to the eucharist than just the eucharistic prayer, the issues encountered there are, it seems to me, so much more serious than with the other parts of the liturgy that I intend to limit my remarks to the eucharistic prayer. Second, the future has never really been my cup of tea.

Nonetheless, I remain convinced that contemporary developments are frequently in reaction, conscious or unconscious, to preconceptions established since A.D. 1000 that have their roots before, even well before, that date. It is in that conviction, in any case, that I dare to proceed. If it should appear that I refuse to address the topic before us and prefer rather to wallow in antiquity, I can only beg your patience and promise to get to the point eventually. My purpose, as will be immediately obvious, is not to provide information that you do not have already, but to stake out some positions on which we can build later, I hope.

THE STRUCTURE OF EUCHARISTIC PRAYERS

At York in 1989 the English Language Liturgical Consultation adopted certain notes toward the possible framing of an ecumenical eucharistic prayer. Those notes, *Some Elements in the Eucharistic Prayer*, provide exactly that, a list and brief description of some elements encountered in eucharistic prayers. Their concern is clearly to be descriptive, and no more than that. While certain of those elements can be presented only in relation to others, these notes do not address the larger question of the structure of the prayer, the issue that is, I would suggest, of the greatest importance. We need to see the prayer as a whole, not as an assembly of elements joined in an order predicated upon unexamined presuppositions. Most of the other questions that face our churches in the framing of eucharistic prayers—questions of linguistic relevance or cultural indigenization or gender specificity or what have you—are independent of this question of structure, and may be dealt with in the appropriate local forum. The same is true of the issue of theological correctness. However, anaphoral structure has itself contributed so much to the eucharistic theology predicated upon it that it is difficult to separate the strands. I hope, nonetheless, that we can at least look at some instances of that interplay between eucharistic theology and anaphoral structure so that we can better assess the importance of the structural question. It is structure, rather than verbal agreement, that has been the medium of tradition.

Even so, of course, there has not been but one structure. What is true, and all the more surprising in view of the variety, is that the eucharistic prayer seems to have begun with thanksgiving or praise, expressed by one or more of a number of praise verbs, and to have moved from that proclamatory section to a supplication. That it need not have been so is clear from a glance at the index of incipits in any of the medieval sacramentaries where we will find a veritable plethora of short prayers of the type that we Anglicans call collects, beginning with supplication right from the top. *Da, quaesumus, omnipotens sempiterne Deus* ... Or, in our more immediate experience, 'Direct us, O Lord, in all our doings ...' While such directly supplicatory formulae abound in the liturgy, folding in a brief address as convenient, thanksgiving in the eucharistic prayer expands the address, setting the basis for the following supplication. This is true already in the very archaic forms in chapter IX of *Didache*, where very simple thanksgivings over the cup and broken bread lead into a supplication for the gathering of the church.[1] As early as the middle of the second century, Justin Martyr suggests that this thanksgiving included reference to creation[2], and that was often referred to the agency of the Second Person, as appears in the primitive form of the Anaphora of St. Mark in Strasbourg pap. 254.[3] In the prayer for the first celebration by a newly ordained bishop in *The Apostolic Tradition*,[4] the opening thanksgiving has become a more or less complete Christological kerygma, and that is the case as well in a later prayer of the same structure attributed to Epiphanius.[5] Indeed, the eucharistic prayer, as has often been noted of late, became the primary liturgical confession of faith long before any creed was added to the liturgy. Even the Aramaic (and Syriac) verb for giving thanks means also to confess.

EUCHARISTIC PRAYER IN EARLY GREEK TRADITION

The prayer in *The Apostolic Tradition* is offered only as a model, as a later passage of that order makes clear. We do not, of course, have the texts of spontaneous prayers modelled on it, or another model, or no model at all; but it seems *The Apostolic Tradition* or its source served as starting point, at least, for a pattern of eucharistic prayer of which many written examples survive in use today. From the earliest form of what we will know as the Anaphora of Basil (perhaps even earlier than his actual association with it) that Christological thanksgiving is preceded by a praise of the Creator that concludes in sanctus.[6] That prayer is frequently spoken of as Cappadocian today, but many still speak of the form it represents as Antiochene, and there is good reason to suspect that the sanctus was first included in the eucharistic prayer in Syria. A later expanded version of Basil and the Anaphora of St. John Chrysostom show the same general structure

---

[1] R. C. D Jasper and C. J. Cuming, *Prayers of the Eucharist: Early and Reformed*, third edition (Pueblo Publishing Company, New York, 1987), 23. [Hereafter cited as *PEER.*]
[2] *First Apology*, 13, although the relevance of this passage to the eucharist is not definite.
[3] *PEER,* 53.
[4] *PEER,* 35.
[5] *PEER,* 142.
[6] *PEER,* 70.

as the Cappadocian prototype of Basil, as do the anaphora in Book VIII of *Apostolic Constitutions* and a number of others. In these Antiochene anaphoras (if we may use that designation), as in that in *The Apostolic Tradition*, the thanksgiving for the work of Christ reaches its climax in the narrative of Christ's institution of the eucharist, a narrative followed at once by a sentence that relates that historical institution to the present act of the Church, combining in one way or another the notions of remembering, offering, and thanksgiving. With that sentence, which we know as the 'anamnesis', the first part of the prayer, the expanded address of thanksgiving, comes to its conclusion, and the prayer turns to supplication.

As early as the very archaic form in *Didache* IX, this supplication is for the gathering of the church. The derivation of these three strophes from Jewish sources has been argued by some[1], but the Jewish forms in question are too uncertain for the time of *Didache*, it seems to me, and I am more impressed with the close structural parallel to the forms following communion in *Didache* X. These seem to many of us to represent a rather conscious revision of a common grace after meals, the basic structure of which is evident already in the second century B.C. in *Jubilees*.[2] The common thread in the many textual variants of the supplication of this grace is concern for the future of Israel, as the supplications in *Didache* IX and X are concerned for the church. When the prayer in *The Apostolic Tradition* turns from thanksgiving to supplication after the anamnesis, the concern is again for the community. Here, however, theological development has introduced a pneumatological element into this ecclesiological concern and the supplication includes an invocation of the Holy Spirit. The text is not without ambiguity, but although we may debate about whether the Holy Spirit is here invoked on the people, or on their act of offering, or on the gifts they offer, it is more than probable that these are distinctions that we bring to the text from later developments, perhaps even quite recent developments.

The second half of this present century has seen the emergence of a distinction between consecratory and sanctificatory invocations of the Holy Spirit, a matter to which we shall return. Let it suffice for the moment to observe that this distinction is foreign to the early history of the liturgy and has been created in order to defend an assessment of the role of the institution narrative that requires closer and more open examination. Supplication for the people in the eucharistic prayer will often (with or without invocation of the Holy Spirit) focus upon the gifts they present, or (still with or without the invocation of the Holy Spirit) it will go beyond the gathered community to intercede for those not present. With happy frequency, it will do both. It is important, nonetheless, to recognize that the admission of pneumatological reference is a development within this supplication. The epiclesis is not merely an item of anaphoral architecture that may be inserted *ad libitum* without further structural implications. When it is encountered, we may be sure that the prayer has moved from praise and thanksgiving, i.e., from proclamation, to supplication.

---

[1] See, e.g., Enrico Mazza, *L'anafora eucaristica: syudi sulle origini*. Bibliotheca «Ephemerides Liturgicae» «Subsidia» 62 (C.L.V.-Edizioni Liturgische, Roma, 1992) 39-44.
[2] *Jubilees* xxii:5-9.

In this Antiochene structure, then, a theological praise of the Creator ending in sanctus leads to a Christological thanksgiving that comes to its climax in the institution narrative and anamnesis and then turns to a supplication with pneumatological reference. In such a structure, the eucharistic prayer manifests the same trinitarian pattern as is evident in baptismal creeds and their more developed conciliar progeny. These latter, and especially the Niceno-Constant-inopolitan formula as reported at Chalcedon, will eventually find a place in the eucharistic liturgy itself. While the time and position of that addition will vary, we may wonder whether such a development is not something of an index to the loss of the eucharistic prayer's preeminent place in the church's kerygma, and its reduction to a prayer of consecration.

In the eucharistic prayers of which we have spoken, all of which appeared originally in Greek (although similar prayers are found in Syriac), this transition from thanksgiving to supplication falls after the institution narrative and anamnesis. It is at that point that we must recognize the structural fulcrum of the prayer. That was not always the case. The form we see in the early Basil, John Fenwick has argued, was eventually melded with a much simpler prayer at Jerusalem to produce the Anaphora of Saint James, one of the well-known Antiochene prayers.[1] The Jerusalem rite that lies behind James, described in Cyril's fifth Mystagogical Catechesis, seems to Fenwick (and Cutrone before him[2]) to have given no place to the institution narrative and anamnesis, and the shift to supplication came quickly after sanctus. If that reading of Cyril prevails, and I currently suspect that it will, such a rite at Jerusalem and its similarities and dissimilarities to other local rites of the period would deserve continuing close study. Even earlier at Alexandria, the primitive core of the Anaphora of St. Mark, preserved in Stras. pap. 254[3], included the shift from proclamation to supplica-tion, and sanctus, institution narrative and anamnesis were later appended to that primitive core, thus falling after the shift to supplication, as did, of course, the epiclesis after the anamnesis. The resulting anaphora, with its extended inter-cessions prior to sanctus, was a very different structure, but one that eventually gave way to Basil itself as the prayer in normal Coptic use. These alternative structures, then, proved to be only temporary exceptions to a growing oriental consensus in which the Antiochene form today reigns almost supreme.

LATIN LITURGICAL TRADITION

However, if such a consensus (now vastly multilingual) came to be enjoyed by what had been a Greek liturgical tradition, it was much different in areas where the liturgical language was Latin. Those who have identified *The Apostolic Tradi-tion* with the liturgical practice of the church in Rome have been hard pressed to relate the eucharistic prayer in that document to the *Canon Missae* so closely

---

[1] John R. K. Fenwick, *The Anaphoras of St. Basil and St. James. Orientalia Christiana Analecta*, 240 (Pontificium Institutum Orientale, Roma, 1992).
[2] E. J. Cutrone, 'Cyril's Mystagogical Catecheses and the Evolution of the Jerusalem Anaphora' in *OCP*, 44 (1978) 52-64.
[3] *PEER*, 52-54.

identified with that church. That is a thankless endeavour, it would seem. Much more to the point, I would suggest, is that over a period in the fourth century that thus far defies closer definition the Church of Rome abandoned the Greek liturgical tradition in favour of the Latin. The fact that the capitular library in Verona has a manuscript of the *Sententiae de Bono* of Isidore of Seville some of whose folios contain in palimpsest the texts of several Church Orders, one of which is that now known as *The Apostolic Tradition*, all in Latin translation, does not indicate the use of a eucharistic prayer from that document in Latin liturgical tradition. Whatever is to be said of Roman liturgy in the third century, it seems likely to have been in Greek, and the change to a Latin eucharistic prayer was not effected, evidently, by translation of the Greek prayer into a different language, but by the adoption of a liturgy already developed in territories where the liturgical language was Latin. The most important of these, North Africa, has regrettably left us no text of the eucharistic prayer. Evidence from northern Italy, while sparse, is nonetheless helpful.

Ambrose, in *De Sacramentis*, distinguishes between the words of the priest and the words of the Lord.[1] Yet, when he sets out to quote the latter, he gives us, in fact, the germ of what, with significant development, we find called *Canon Actionis* in the Gelasian Sacramentary. His characterization of the preceding words of the bishop suggests that these, too, included a part of what would later be known as the Canon: 'praise is offered to God; prayer is made for the people, for kings, for others . . .' These prayers seem very like the intercessions we will encounter later in *Te igitur.* As for the offering of praise to God, however, we have no such fixed text to which we can point. Rather, as appears from the Arian fragments published by Cardinal Mai,[2] the praise of God was variable, continuing the tradition of extempore prayer. Those two examples come from Ambrose's general environment, temporal and geographical. The collection we call the Leonine or Veronese Sacramentary is more recent, but many of the formulae contained in it could belong to the century following Ambrose. Every mass there contains one prayer that begins *Vere dignum.* In many if not most cases these give no indication of moving directly into sanctus, and it is commonly supposed that these antedate the Latin adoption of that hymn. These, clearly, are such *praefationes* as the two cited by Mai's anonymous Arian. The thanksgiving or praise, in other words, continued to be composed by the bishop, although it was committed to written form more frequently from the fourth century. The part of the eucharistic prayer more likely to remain the same from one celebration to the next was entirely supplicatory, and it was in that supplicatory environment that one recited the charter narrative, by contrast to its situation within a thanksgiving for the work of Christ such as we have seen in Greek tradition. Therefore, in neither *De Sacramentis* nor the later form of the canon does the immediately following anamnesis include a reiteration of the thanksgiving theme such as is commonly found in the Greek anaphoras. If, in Greek tradition,

---

[1] *PEER,* 144f.
[2] A. Häggai-I. Pahl, *Prex Eucharistica.* (Spicilegium Friburgense, 12, Fribourg Suisse, 1968), 422. The second of these fragments appears in translation in *PEER,* 156f.

the thanksgiving became a major locus for the proclamation of the faith, this Latin tradition that was to be so formative in western liturgical history allowed for that kerygmatic function only piecemeal, at best, in the much more limited and variable *Vere dignum* formulae, roughly equivalent to what we know today as proper prefaces. The fixed body of prayer, including the institution narrative and anamnesis, has nothing of thanksgiving, and in the West much more than in the East this prayer came to be thought of and spoken of as 'the prayer of consecration'.

One might wonder what it was that encouraged Ambrose to overlook the historical character of the narrative and treat it, rather, as though it were concerned with the consecration of the gifts on the table. Roughly contemporary with Ambrose, John Chrysostom, while insisting on the importance of the epiclesis that would follow, nonetheless recognized the defining role of the words of Christ.[1] Certainly, theological articulation of eucharistic consecration was drawing increasing attention in the later fourth century, and that was still understood to be tied in some way to the liturgical tradition. The liturgical tradition, however, was often more conservative than theological discourse regarding eucharistic consecration. The fixed prayer known to Ambrose, indeed, prayed before the narrative for the acceptance of the offering, not, as would the later Roman Canon, 'that it may be unto us' the body and blood of the Lord, but rather, 'because it is the figure of the body and blood of our Lord Jesus Christ.' Such a liturgical expression offered little help to a teacher concerned to communicate the current theology. In any case, Ambrose's argument from the narrative to make a mystagogical point to his Milanese neophytes took on, as we know, a life of its own. By the twelfth century the view that the words of Christ themselves effected consecration was general in the West, and Pére Gy has cited medieval texts that insist that only these words are necessary to complete the sacrament.[2] All the rest of the eucharistic prayer is hardly more than literary decoration. While that opinion failed to win the field, the way was nonetheless prepared for Luther's views expressed so pungently in his *Formula Missae*: 'From here on almost everything smacks and savours of sacrifice. And the words of life and salvation are imbedded in the midst of it all, just as the ark of the Lord once stood in the idol's temple next to Dagon. . . . Let us therefore repudiate everything that smacks of sacrifice, together with the entire canon and retain only that which is pure and holy, and so order our mass.'[3]

EUCHARISTIC PRAYER IN THE REFORMATION
Luther's reaction against the notion of eucharistic sacrifice, and that of Cranmer, was extreme, perhaps, but understandable in their historical context. It is hard to know what they would have made of the sacrificial language predicated on Malachi 1.11 in such early texts as *Didache* XIV and the Strasbourg papyrus. Melancthon, it seems, was much more tolerant of the notion of sacrifice as he found it in Greek anaphoras. That, however, was another world than that which

---

[1] *De resurrect. mortuorum 8; De proditione Judae* 1,6.
[2] Pierre-Marie Gy, *La liturgie dans l'histoire* (Editions du Cerf, Paris, 1990) 214-215.
[3] PEER, 191-192.

confronted Luther and Cranmer. The eucharistic sacrifice of which their own theological formation had spoken and against which they rebelled was almost certainly that summarized by Gabriel Biel, first Professor of Theology at Tübingen, in his large explication of the *Canon Missae* in the fifteenth century. Based on a highly realistic doctrine of consecration that was focused on the *verba Christi* in the institution narrative, he followed others of his time in drawing the obvious conclusion that what was offered to the Father by the priest in the following anamnesis, *Unde et memores,* was nothing less than the very Body and Blood of the Lord.[1] Nothing I have read of the reformers suggests that they were aware that the general acceptance of that doctrine among Catholics was a relatively recent development. The sixteenth century was not a good time for historical-critical studies. In the thirteenth century, however, Thomas Aquinas had insisted that the eucharist is first offered as a sacrifice, and then consecrated and received as a sacrament. For that reason, he limited the sacrificial aspect of the eucharist to the preparation of the altar with its variable prayer over the oblations. The canon he treated as only a prayer of consecration, effected by the words of Christ in the narrative. Given that, he has as little to say of offering in the following anamnesis as would Cranmer.[2] His, however, was not the theological world that confronted Cranmer. Indeed, in that world in which communion of the people had become increasingly infrequent, not a few probably saw the purpose of the consecration as provision of a worthy victim for the sacrifice. Little wonder, then, that Cranmer, even in his first step of 1549, having strengthened the old *Quam oblationem* before the narrative with an invocation of 'thy Word and Holy Spirit', would omit from the anamnesis after the narrative any mention whatsoever of offering the gifts. The rite of 1552 went much further, of course, and effectively incorporated the act of communion itself into the eucharistic prayer at the point previously occupied by the anamnesis. The ingenuity of that initiative, an almost flawless expression of Cranmer's Swiss theology, was vitiated by Elizabeth I, but in 1559 and 1662 the structure of the prayer preceding communion remained the same: dialogue, preface, sanctus, supplication with an expanded address, and institution narrative. The restructuring represented by the so-called 'Interim Rite' following the debacle of 1928 reflected the desire for a fully developed eucharistic prayer, and it is still that quest that brings us here.

Those developments in England, of course, were not the only game in town during the seventeenth and eighteenth centuries. The Scottish 1637 reprise of 1549 was reissued in 1722 and appeared again, with strengthened oblation, in 1735. Only after the posthumous publication of Thomas Rattray's *Ancient Liturgy of the Church of Jerusalem* did the Scottish Liturgy return the shift from thanksgiving to supplication (i.e., the epiclesis) to a point after the anamnesis,

---

[1] Gabriel Biel, *Canonis Missae expositio*, Heiko A. Oberman and Wm. J. Courtney, editors (Weisbaden, 1965) Part 2, lect. 54 [Vol. 1, 335-344, especially 340-342].

[2] *Summa Theologica* III.83.4. Of the anamnesis, Thomas says (after discussing the institution narrative), only, 'Thirdly, he makes excuse for his presumption in obeying Christ's command, saying: *Unde et memores, etc. . . .*'

following the lead taken by Bishop Falconar's 'Wee Bookie' of 1755. It was that Scottish Liturgy of 1764 that Samuel Seabury sought to establish in Connecticut following his consecration and it was substantially that form of eucharistic prayer that was adopted, with influence from both Seabury and a number of clergy of Scottish background, in the first Prayer Book of the Church in the United States in 1789. These eighteenth century Anglican prayers retained the variable prefaces of western tradition, but otherwise turned to the pattern argued for in Nonjuror patristic studies, a pattern that would, a century and a half later, come to light in *The Apostolic Tradition*. That setting of the fulcrum of the eucharistic prayer, the point of transition from thanksgiving to supplication, between anamnesis and epiclesis has taken deep root in North America and looms large today in the liturgies of both the Episcopal Church and the Anglican Church of Canada. Also, *The Book of Common Order* of the Church of Scotland (1940, 1979) has adopted this same pattern, including in its anamnesis the significant phrase, 'pleading his eternal Sacrifice'; and Bryan Spinks has traced the anamnesis-epiclesis order in Presbyterian use back to the Canadian Presbyterian *Book of Common Order* of 1922.[1] In the Church of England, so far as I am aware, this structure has appeared only as an alternative in the ill-fated revision of 1928.

NEW EUCHARISTIC PRAYERS IN OUR OWN DAY
Contemporary exercises in the framing of eucharistic prayers were given fresh impetus in the rash of liturgical reform that has marked our time, and especially the past three decades. In Roman Catholic reform, the Concilium for the Implementation of the Second Vatican Council's Constitution on the Liturgy proposed three new eucharistic prayers that mark a decisive departure from the concerns of the old *Canon missae*, retained as the first eucharistic prayer. These reflect in different ways the desire to restore the element of thanksgiving proclamation. In the case of the first of them (Prayer II) a fixed paraphrase of the opening thanksgiving from *The Apostolic Tradition* leads into sanctus, while the third new prayer (Prayer IV) reflects some significant dependency upon Antiochene models. In contrast to those progenitors, nonetheless, the institution narrative forms no part of the Christological kerygma that provides the substance of the thanksgiving. Rather, the transition to the request, the supplication, is made before the institution narrative. This takes the form of an invocation of the Holy Spirit for the consecration of the gifts, and was seen as necessary for the maintenance of the specifically Roman character of the prayers. This was viewed, to quote Annibale Bugnini, as, *cosa, tra tutte le altre, la pi · tipica della tradizione romana*[2], already established in the Roman Canon by the petition

---

[1] Bryan D. Spinks, 'The ascension and the Vicarious Humanity of Christ: The Christology and Soteriology Behind the Church of Scotland's Anamnesis and Epiklesis,' in J. Neil Alexander, (editor) *Time and Community*, (The Pastoral Press, Washington, D.C., 1990), 187. In a personal communication, Spinks assures me that the date of this BCO should be, in fact, 1932.
[2] Annibale Bugnini, *La riforma liturgica* (1948-1975) Bibliotheca «Ephemerides Liturgicae» «Subsidia» (C.L.V.-Editione Liturgische, Roma, 1983) 444.

Quam oblationem, although it made no reference to the Holy Spirit. Indeed, the nearest equivalent to that petition in the *De Sacramentis* of Ambrose, *Fac nobis*, cannot even be called a petition for the consecration of the gifts, as we noted earlier. Nonetheless, such has been the strength of the supposition that it is the institution narrative that effects consecration that the shift from thanksgiving to supplication, the fulcrum point of the prayer, now falls prior to that narrative in the new Roman anaphoras, and so puts the narrative in a supplication context rather than the thanksgiving in which it is found in Greek tradition. In spite of that, the anamnesis in these new Roman prayers returns to thanksgiving as do the Greek, unlike the Roman Canon which, having already after sanctus shifted to supplication, made no further mention of thanksgiving in the anamnesis. Further, conscious of the Greek tradition's invocation of the Spirit following the anamnesis, the new Roman prayers have a further epiclesis at that point, this time focused on the communicants. It is this bifurcation of the epiclesis that brought forth the totally untraditional distinction between consecratory and sanctificatory 'epicleses' referred to above. This utterly novel distinction succeeds only in obscuring more serious structural questions that, sadly, do not seem to be open to discussion in Roman Catholic circles where the Latin Rite is concerned, although the alternative structure we have noted as Greek is accepted by the Roman Church in all its oriental rites, be they Byzantine, Coptic, Syrian or Armenian. In sum, these new Roman prayers have attempted to incorporate the structural clarity of the Antiochene anaphoras while at the same time distorting that structure fundamentally through inserting an epiclesis before the narrative and so turning from thanksgiving to supplication from that point, only to switch back to thanksgiving in the anamnesis and to supplication again for the so-called 'sanctificatory' epiclesis. The result, when compared to classical structures of East or West, is institutionalized vacillation.

Beyond that matter of structural confusion, the identification of the institution narrative as focus of a consecration realistically conceived raises the possibility, noted earlier in the thought of Gabriel Biel, that the *offerimus* in the anamnesis will be understood to refer to the priest at the altar directly offering the unique sacrifice of Christ by presenting his body and blood to the Father. That view has, in Roman Catholic tradition, received perhaps its most unfortunate expression in the anamnesis of Eucharistic Prayer IV of the Missal of Paul VI. In a formulation utterly novel to the tradition, and one that has received withering criticism from Roman Catholic liturgists, the celebrant prays (in the ICEL translation):

'Father, we now celebrate this memorial of our redemption. We recall Christ's death, his descent among the dead, his resurrection, and his ascension to your right hand; and, looking forward to his coming in glory, we offer you his body and blood, the acceptable sacrifice which brings salvation to the whole world.'

The Latin text is: '*offerimus tibi eius Corpus et Sanguinem*'. In a personal communication some months ago, Fr. Joseph Gelineau, who was responsible for framing the original project for this prayer and presenting it to the drafting group, wrote that he did not know where, when or how this unfortunate expression entered the text, and suggests that those questions might be answered only by delving into the archives of the Concilium and tracking later stages of revision. It should be added that the ICEL translation quoted above has itself been altered recently. In the forthcoming revision of the Missal the relevant lines are: 'we offer you the sacrifice of his body and blood, an offering pleasing to you, which brings salvation to all the world,' and a note in the final report adds, 'The wording of these lines has been slightly revised in keeping with the more "sacramental" mode of expression long established in the traditional eucharistic prayer.'[1] While that will not correct the all too plain language of the Latin *editio tipica*, it is gratifying to know that those responsible for pastoral implementation are cognizant of the problems such expression presents.

For many Anglicans the problem is quite the opposite and, I suspect, for the same structural reason. However the consecration may be conceived theologically, much of our tradition has reflected a serious diffidence toward using the expression, 'we offer', in the following anamnesis. That diffidence continues to dog the steps of a great many Anglicans to our own day, though some seem to have found relief through translating *offere* instead of transliterating it. Nonetheless, 'to offer,' whether it is rendering *ob fere* or, *prospherein* surely means nothing very different from 'to set before'. What is more important than such verbal nicety, I suspect, is to note and treat with great seriousness the evidence that this anxiety over eucharistic sacrifice is most severe among us where it is accompanied by insistence on prayer for the consecration of the gifts prior to the institution narrative. The price of a consecratory epiclesis before the narrative seems, for many Anglicans, to be agonizing ambivalence regarding oblation in the anamnesis following the narrative. Where oblation precedes any supplication for the consecration of the gifts (where, that is, the single epiclesis follows the anamnesis), reference to sacrifice seems not to produce the lamentable polarization that plagues so much of Anglican liturgical thought. That this is not a catholic *versus* reformed issue is made plain by *The Book of Common Order* of the Church of Scotland to which reference was made earlier . . .

What, then, is it that is really at issue here? Yes, from 1549 through 1662 and beyond, the English *Book of Common Prayer*, following to this extent the structure of the Roman Canon, limited its thanksgiving proclamation to the preface, and the following sanctus formed the fulcrum, the dividing point, between that thanksgiving and the supplication. That supplication included prayer that we would be partakers of his most blessed Body and Blood, either because the bread and wine had been blessed and sanctified by Word and Holy Spirit or because we receive them according to his institution in remembrance of his death and passion. While not all would agree that what this petition envisions should even be characterized as 'consecration,' there seems to be a broader consensus that, whatever it says or means, it should precede the institution narrative. In such a

---

[1] International Committee on English in the Liturgy, *Third Progress Report on the Revision of the Roman Missal* (Washington, D.C., 1992) 93.

general structure, that is understandable, especially when the distribution of communion follows immediately upon the narrative. But when, as in our own day, there is concern to return to a fuller thanksgiving proclamation of the work of Christ within the body of the prayer following sanctus, the rationale for shifting to supplication before the narrative, and so excluding the institution of the eucharist from our thanksgiving, is more difficult to understand.

At this point, it may be that there is nothing for it but to open the desperate issue of the 'moment of consecration'. Bob Taft loves to say that this is not a liturgical question, but a mathematical question. Surely most today would want to say that it is the entire eucharistic prayer that consecrates? Given my preference, I would probably want to go further and say that the identification of the material of communion with the Body and Blood of Christ is something that occurs within the liturgy as a whole. However, our Anglican peculiarity of providing forms for supplemental consecration might make that difficult to sustain. In any case, before we let ourselves be led down the primrose path of choosing between the institution narrative and the epiclesis as the precise point of consecration, we would do well to remember that neither of these finds a place in our earliest eucharistic prayers. Beyond the very early evidence, Jerusalem, it now seems, managed to live without the institution narrative until late in the fourth century, and Rome got along without an epiclesis until 1968. Given our ecumenical responsibility, I would not conclude from such data that either the narrative or the invocation of the Spirit is to be considered a frivolous addition to the pure tradition. But such data might give us the courage to look on them, and much else, with a lighter burden of presupposition, and enable us to look more critically at some of the fashions of the moment.

One of those is the popular acclamation that so commonly today separates the historical narrative from the anamnesis that relates it to the present act of worship. We are told repeatedly that this enrichment has ample precedent in the oriental liturgies. Certainly in these days involvement of the people in the liturgy is an unquestionably good thing, but more careful examination of oriental liturgies reveals that there is more to be said.

The original popular acclamation, evidently, was the *Amen* noted by Justin Martyr,[1] and that has remained important to our own day. In virtually all liturgies since the fifth century, there has been a further interjection, the angelic hymn, sanctus, though it is not always easy to know when and where it was truly popular rather than clericalized. At Rome, sanctus marked the fulcrum between the variable thanksgiving and the supplicatory canon. In oriental liturgies, if some generalization may be allowed, sanctus came at the end of a theological praise and was followed by the Christological thanksgiving.

In Byzantine tradition, that thanksgiving concludes in the anamnesis, and a further acclamation marks the fulcrum on which turns the shift from thanksgiving to supplication: 'We praise thee, we bless thee, we give thanks unto thee, O Lord, and we pray unto thee, O our God,' as Florence Hapgood renders it.[2]

---

[1] *First Apology* 65.
[2] Service Book of the Holy Orthodox-Catholic Apostolic Church. Revised Edition (Syrian Antiochian Orthodox Archdiocese, New York, 1956) 105.

Somewhat more briefly, the choir had also sung Amen after both the bread word and the cup word during the narrative, but it is sanctus before the Christological thanksgiving and this further acclamation marking the shift from anamnesis to epiclesis, from thanksgiving to supplication, that stakes out, so to speak, the tripartite structure of the anaphoras of St. Basil and of St. John Chrysostom. The multiplication of further congregational interjections among some of the pre-chalcedonian churches tends to obscure that structure. Among the Copts, for example, from sanctus on, the anaphora of Basil is virtually a three-voiced fugue between celebrant, the deacon and the congregation who repeat, 'we believe' or 'amen' after almost every sentence uttered by the priest. The text cited for the Byzantine rite just now comes after the anamnesis also in the Coptic Basil, but the same text also precedes the anamnesis, where it concludes a popular confession of the paschal mystery.

However, if I am not terribly mistaken, it was the liturgy of St. James as observed by the Syrian Jacobites on the Malabar coast of India that was destined to have such strong impact on western liturgies in these past few decades. E. C. Ratcliff, of blessed memory, drafted (with J. C. Winslow and others) the distinctive liturgy for the Indian Church published in 1920. Reprinted and revised several times before its appearance as 'A Liturgy for India' in *A Proposed Prayer Book* (1951), this most oriental of Anglican eucharistic prayers seems clearly to reflect the influence of Syrian tradition in India. Here, as in that tradition, we find a popular confession of the paschal mystery before the anamnesis, and, after it, a further popular acclamation: 'We give thanks to thee, we praise thee, we glorify thee, and we pray thee to show thy mercy upon us, and to hearken unto the voice of our prayer,' leading into the epiclesis.[1] It is but slightly variant versions of those popular acclamations that appear again before and following the anamnesis in the liturgy of the Church of South India in 1950 and 1954.[2]

It is my conjecture that it was the great popularity of that South India rite among liturgists in Europe that insinuated into our discourse the possibility and the desirability of adding such a popular acclamation within the eucharistic prayer. However, because the second of those acclamations formed the bridge from the anamnesis to an epiclesis that in the Roman model must precede the institution narrative, it fell victim to that stronger need. Therefore, the only popular acclamation that lived on in recent western revisions was that between the narrative and the anamnesis. What seems not to have been considered adequately, if at all, is that this acclamation, like sanctus before it, would eventually receive musical treatment, and that such treatment would tend to heighten the prominence of the acclamation and make it seem a major punctuation point in the prayer. In fact, with or without music, it does punctuate the anaphora; and, in so doing, it forces a wedge between the narrative and anamnesis that leaves the narrative isolated as an historical account with only seriously diminished continuity with the action of the gathered community that has been, in almost every classical instance since *The Apostolic Tradition*, the expression of the present act of

---

[1] Bernard Wigan, ed., *The Liturgy in English* (Oxford, London, 1962) 103.
[2] *Ibid.* 215.

obedience that brings the narrative to fulfilment. Ligier believed that the institution narrative and anamnesis entered eucharistic prayer tradition as a unit, and to date I know of no evidence that would contradict him. Yet we, with the most laudable of pastoral motives, have forced a wedge into that unit, creating the impression that a third and final section of the eucharistic prayer runs from anamnesis to doxology.

This structural disfunction of the acclamation is beginning to be recognized, and that popular intervention has been placed after the anamnesis in the Roman Catholic eucharistic prayers for Masses with Children. Anglican revisions in the U.S. and Canada include versions of A Common Eucharistic Prayer, an ecumenically drafted anaphora closely modelled upon the Egyptian Basil, and these, leaving the connection between narrative and anamnesis unbroken, have such an acclamation after anamnesis as we noted for the Byzantine tradition, an acclamation that marks the fulcrum on which turns the shift from thanksgiving to supplication. Even where, as in the Roman children's masses, that shift has been made earlier, if there is reason for having but a single acclamation in the body of the prayer, I would hope that it would be positioned after the anamnesis rather than before it. My fear is that current popular practice encourages in forgetfulness (if not violation) of the institution narrative's historical character.

THE THEME OF CREATION

One matter of anaphoral content that is of concern in our time also presents structural problems. This is the doctrine of creation. As noted earlier, the opening praise of God in the Antiochene anaphoras has often been described as 'Theological.' It is, if I can remember Ligier's expression correctly, a praise of God as he is in himself or as creator. Now that I think of it, I'm not comfortable with that memory. Nonetheless, while we cannot say that the opening section of the Antiochene anaphora, between dialogue and sanctus, is always explicitly focused on creation, that is the part of the Antiochene prayers that is most likely to make place for the praise of the creator, by contrast to the more soteriological thanksgiving after sanctus. Western tradition, on the other hand, at least from the Gregorian sacramentaries of the ninth century, found itself shaping the opening variable section of the prayer to a liturgical year that was by that time clearly Christological in its content. These proper prefaces, changing with the feasts and seasons, have become a well-loved feature of our eucharistic prayers. Some of the new prayers, Anglican and Roman, have experimented with a fixed preface, and sometimes this strongly reflects the fundamental doctrine of creation. In other cases, new proper prefaces, especially some for ordinary Sundays, are focused on creation. In still other cases, the body of the thanksgiving after sanctus will include reference to creation. It is certain that if we are to see the eucharistic prayer as once again a primary proclamation of faith, creation must find a prominent place in such a prayer. I would go further, and argue that the eucharistic prayer can most appropriately fulfil that kerygmatic function if it follows the tripartite or Trinitarian structure of the baptismal formula, as do the prayers of Antiochene structure. At the same time, I recognize that the proper prefaces have a respectable tradition in their favour. Even Ratcliff, drafting the overtly oriental Bombay liturgy, bowed to the force of that tradition and retained the variable prefaces. Here again, we could do worse than to look to the Church of Scotland, whose *Book of Common Order* simply expands the common preface to afford a rather full statement on creation, while still leaving room for the insertion of a proper preface. That, I would suggest, is likely to prove more satisfying in the end than is the often less than convincing insinuation of an allusion to creation at some point after sanctus, in a context that is primarily soteriological.

CONCLUSIONS

A simple conclusion, unfortunately, is not easy to produce in a very orderly fashion. Let me, therefore, simply offer a few propositions that may at least initiate further discussion.

1. There is not and is unlikely to be one Anglican eucharistic prayer. That dream (or nightmare, if your prefer) died in the reign of Charles I. Despite an eclipse of the result lasting almost a century, the hope of but one Use would never again escape challenge, and today seems safely out of the question. More important in our own day is whether we can agree on the purpose or purposes of eucharistic prayer.
2. Given our history, it seems that a significant division between our rites focuses on the role we assign to the institution narrative. How and why that narrative is attached to the anamnesis and the relation of such a narrative-anamnesis unit to supplication for consecration (almost surely expressed as an invocation of the Spirit) are questions that follow upon our understanding of the role of the narrative itself. Those questions will not receive the address they deserve, I suspect, until we are of a common mind regarding the role of the narrative.
3. We are unlikely, I would guess, to arrive quickly at theological consensus on the whole question of eucharistic sacrifice. Nonetheless, we should be able to lower the polemical heat regarding reference to the gifts in the anamnesis. What is wanted here is not an agreed expression, but a sufficiently searching examination of the issues to allow us to respect a variety of expression.
4. My own plea would be for serious address to the structure of the prayer, not just to the elements that are likely to be encountered in it. For that, I would submit, we need to look analytically at the tradition in all its variety. Such an analysis, I believe, will reveal a rather consistent pattern of thanksgiving followed by supplication, i.e., eucharist and prayer. If we could agree on that, then we could be sure that we are addressing a single task, and that itself should serve the harder questions of the contents of each of those, while leaving space for wide-ranging variety.

Finally, allow me to say that I am deeply gratified that the Consultation is giving to this matter the attention that it so sorely deserves and needs. Whatever the success or frustration of the enterprise, the church will survive. That assurance, however, does not absolve us of responsibility for what we know, and that is rather more than it was four centuries ago, but probably rather less than it will be only a generation in the future. I wish you all godspeed and good luck in the coming Consultation. I, on the other hand, am retired.

2. Future Directions for Eucharistic Revisions

by Colin Buchanan

THE PAN-ANGLICAN BACKGROUND OF REVISIONS

There have been various attempts in the last four decades to give advice to the whole Anglican Communion on both official and unofficial levels concerning the revision of eucharistic texts. The issue has only arisen as a Pan-Anglican one since 1950, because up until the Lambeth Conference of 1948, the 1662 Prayer Book in its various editions was still treated as a symbol of the bonding of the Communion. By the time of Lambeth 1958 the situation was changed, and two members of the sub-group that worked on liturgical revision were symbolic of that change. One was Colin Dunlop, then Dean of Lincoln, who chaired the Church of England's Liturgical Commission, which had come into being less than three years before and by its existence betokened a prospect of impending liberty in England to authorize new texts. The other was Leslie Brown, then Bishop of Uganda, who was secretary of the group, and had behind him the experience of serving on the Committee which produced the first eucharistic texts of the Church of South India. A large part of the recommendations of the group reflected principles on which the South India Liturgy had been created, and I have attempted elsewhere to spell out both the dependence of the group on South India, and the later effects of the same principles on *A Liturgy for Africa* and the first pan-Anglican structure document.[1]

There are two 'structure documents', dating from 1965 and 1969. The first arose from Lambeth 1958, and was produced by four persons, with Leslie Brown, then Archbishop of Uganda, responsible for the drafting.[2] The second arose from a consultation on liturgy which followed the Lambeth Conference in August 1968, and was drafted by Ronald Jasper and Leslie Brown, by that time Bishop of St. Edmundsbury and Ipswich. The two documents give but broad guidance that reflect current liturgical thought concerning structure.[3]

There are two other contributions worth noting. In October 1983 a sub-group of the Primates' Meeting drafted a statement for ACC-6, the meeting of the Anglican Consultative Council scheduled for 1984 in Lagos. The Primates had been considering whether the introduction of new eucharistic liturgies affected the Communion's traditional sense of identity. The sub-group wrote a report on

---

[1] See my *Modern Anglican Liturgies, 1958-1968,* (Oxford, 1968) pp.8-21 for a treatment of the effects of Lambeth 1958 on revised Anglican Liturgies. The liturgies are cross-referenced.

[2] See my *Further Anglican Liturgies 1968-1975,* (Grove Books, 1975) pp.27-31.

[3] Thus the 1969 statement suggests the use of the daily offices as the liturgy of the word, but is too early to locate the exchange of the peace with any certainty.

the question 'How does the Anglican Communion retain its traditional sense of identity?' I was asked to write a report on 'Liturgy in the Anglican Communion from 1973 to 1984', and I was to take this sub-group document into partiuclar account. This report was itself to go to the Lagos meeting.[1]

Finally, the bishops returned to the issue at the 1988 Lambeth Conference, and a section to which I acted as secretary worked on principles of liturgical renewal. We did not, however, address details of the revision of liturgical texts, and frankly gave little attention to the eucharist. Along with a treatment of larger flexibility, and of linguistic and inculturation issues, we had one paragraph on 'Eucharist: Meeting and Mission':

'203. We do not attempt here to discuss technicalities of the eucharistic rites. Instead we note that in the eucharist the Church unites in the praises of God, receives God's holy word, expresses her life in the Spirit, sustains the mutual fellowship of her members, recommits herself to Almighty God, and, from this holy feast, returns to the world to fulfil God's mission. The eucharist is a locus for mutual sharing and ministry for the "building up" of the Church (1 Cor. 14). The eucharist may include: various teaching methods to minister the word, drama, dance, extemporary prayer, groups for study or intercession, healing ministries, weddings, and other public activities of the local Christian community. Christian mission is itself vitiated if the Church's eucharistic practice does not in fact build up the people of God.'[2]

This was followed by a brief mention of agapes or love feasts (para 204), and of presidency at communion (para 205) and of lay distributants (para 206).

These minor initiatives in the revision of the eucharist are set out at the beginning of this paper, not only to demonstrate that they are in fact few and unambitious, but also to emphasize that they are, almost without exception, the work of bishops. Yet, however rare these contributions to liturgical revision are, and however concentrated in the episcopal stratum they might be, they stand in contrast to the almost complete absence of any work on the subject done on a pan-Anglican basis by liturgists.

LITURGISTS GET TOGETHER

Obviously, there existed by 1993 a secure, if skeletal, structure for International Anglican Liturgical Consultations, including the affirmation and recognition by the joint meeting of the Primates and the ACC at Cape Town in January 1993. The Consultations were true gatherings of liturgists, from all six continents. By 1991 there had been four full Consultations, one every two years since 1985. The 1985 and 1991 meetings had handled initiation questions, the 1987 meeting, issues of the role of the laity in worship (along with questions of the structure of

---

[1] This report was made available to the Primates at ACC-6 in 1984, but it was not published at that time. It is presently published in my *Anglican Eucharistic Liturgy, 1975-1985* (Grove Liturgical Study no. 41, Grove Books, Bramcote, 1985) pp.24-32.

[2] *The Truth Shall Make You Free: The Lambeth Conference 1988* (Church House Publishing, 1989) p.73. See also my *Lambeth and Liturgy 1988* (Grove Worship Series no. 106, Grove Books, Bramcote, 1989) pp.20-21.

IALCs), and the 1989 one the problem of inculturation. The eucharist had not been considered in itself at all, but was put on the agenda for the next full IALC at Dublin in 1995. The fact that revision of the eucharist is on the agenda for Dublin will itself serve as an introduction to Untermarchtal.

At this delightful spot in south Germany thirty liturgists gathered in August 1993 to consider not so much the content of future revision of the eucharist, but, to identify issues to be discussed and to delineate principles from which revised eucharistic liturgies might derive their content, in preparation for a full discussion at the 1993 Dublin Consultation (IALC-5).

PROVIDING PRINCIPLES FOR REVISION

I have to begin by issuing some warnings:

(i) We have no guarantee that the future will be like the past—a principle I learned when reading philosophy as an undergraduate. It is always possible that we are at or near the end of Anglican ways of gradual change, and are about to face a fundamental liturgical revolution. On the other hand, however fragile the evidence may be, the past is the only place where the evidence of trends, principles, or laws of liturgical revision can be found. But the warning about the future must be given.

(ii) I must also emphasize that in my own person I make no definitive or authoritative staement. This arises not only from awareness of the limitations of any Consultation; nor only from proper humility in relation to the future. In my own person I would in any case want to avoid pontificating, and my method has been to try to create a map, and leave others to indicate the way to take through the country thus identified.

(iii) In any case Anglicanism has in each province total provincial independence and autonomy; and the various provinces are prey to both uncritical conformity (i.e. attempts to be like others, especially where there is lack of academic and creative confidence locally), and are also to eccentric whim (i.e. the power of advocacy of one or two powerful voices in places which lack self-confidence). Over and above that there is often also a tension between provincial legislative bodies and parish experience and needs.

POSITIVE PRINCIPLES FOR LITURGICAL REVISION

With those warnings, I turn to positive principles. There is a great range, and I wish not so much to expound or recommend (though I have my own scale of value-judgments) as simply to chart some of what seem to me to be the most important principles by which revision might be shaped.

So I proceed with a review of past events, sometimes past controversies, which might be viewed as establishing principles:

(a) The institution of the Lord's Supper: the scriptural accounts of the Institution must be in view. (The Last Supper must, of course, have been related to principles provided from its own background; were there, for instance, principles derived from the passover meal? Or is the crucial principle the uniqueness of the incarnate Son of God, the unprecedented character of his saving work, and the impossibility of laying down lines from before his era to which he had to conform?). In more general terms, we must have a line of some authority which exhibits the controlling character of scripture. As Anglicans, we want (I trust) to say that nothing can be ordered in liturgy which is contrary to holy writ, though that still leaves us with (i) the *prima facie* claims of that which has taken a strong and persevering place in history, and (ii) the difficulty created by the lack of liturgical models in scripture. I suspect that even the most determined believer in the principle of *sola scriptura* would be hard put to show why his or her particular liturgical text must prevail as the best expression of scriptural truth.

(b) Historical evidence from the first century to the sixteenth: This heading is the most complex and diverse one imaginable. A vast tract of historical literature, archaeology and art must come under review. Whatever the value of 'primitive tradition', there will be a demanding and scholarly procedure required to recover it. And, when the distinguishing features of the eucharist in this place, or that century, have been fairly confidently identified, the exact degree of authority any one answer holds for us today is still up for discussion.

(c) The Reformation concern for the purpose of the rite: when the reformers inherited the rite, they discerned its inherited central purposes to be, firstly, a tightly defined consecration which would lead to a quasi-localized presence of Christ; and, secondly, the offering of an impetratory (or even propitiatory) sacrifice. The texts may have read slightly differently, but the rationales surrounding the rite were so strident that they had to be treated as one with it. They in turn wrote liturgies that would lead to a single end-result in the reception of communion. This was of course an outworking of a concern for the supremacy of scripture, but the Reformation divide was both expressed and focussed in doctrines of the eucharist itself, and the changes to the eucharist became standards against which further attempts at revision were judged.

(d) In the seventeenth and eighteenth centuries Anglicans gave a new value to the actual primitive rites to which they had access. This is not a visible feature of 1662 itself, a rite which remained in principle Cranmerian and yet managed to claim that it was reviving the worship of the early church! But the Scottish sequence of revision from 1637 onwards saw a growing fascination with actual ancient texts. The 1764 rite—and thus the American 1790 rite—were really revisions of Cranmer's principles. In the process a particular feature of the ancient Eastern liturgies, which wee being treated by drafters as not only primitive but even apostolic, came into prominence. This feature was the epiclesis, or invocation of the Spirit upon the elements, after the narrative of institution and the (restored) anamnesis. This predilection may accordingly be summarized: 'authoritative means primitive; primitive means Eastern; Eastern means that the epiclesis should be in the particular form, and in the particular place in the eucharistic prayer that the 1764 rite exhibits.'

(e) The nineteenth and twentieth century dependence upon Roman Catholic usage: the second generation of anglo-catholics in the nineteenth century found their own principles of catholicism orientated them, almost inevitably, towards Rome. Rome was the centre of Catholic unity, the seat of Catholic authority, the test of Catholic truth. Once an Anglican priest or indeed a whole movement was itching to 'enrich' the eucharist in a catholic way, the principal sources of enrichment were medieval England or modern Rome—and it is least possible that the strand of romanticism which imbued the catholic revival, whilst it paid lip-service to both medievalism and Englishness, found in the long run a deeper and more measurable satisfaction in practising modern ultramontanism. In England the outworkings of this principle were to be found in the years from 1860 to the 1930s largely in unofficial developments, such as extra-liturgical devotions to the Blessed Sacrament, the re-introduction of water-bread, the adoption of advanced ceremonial, and interpolation of liturgical material from medieval or modern Roman Catholic sources into Anglican worship services. In some places overseas these principles had an even greater effect than they did in England. Rites with a heavy dependance upon Rome, though in African vernacular tongues, became in the first quarter of this century the official diocesan rites of Zanzibar, Nyasaland, and Northern Rhodesia.

The Liturgical Movement reforms within the Roman Catholic church undermined the ultramontanism that may have motivated revision of eucharistic text and practice that was inspired by anglo-catholicism. In general the use of Rome's modern texts in Anglicanism has usually nowadays to be defended on the basis of their intrinsic merits (or occasionally as a means of ecumenical pathfinding), rather than simply on the *a priori* grounds of their source.

(f) The twentieth century conflict concerning the means of consecration: this issue was present in the eighteenth century in the contrast between 1662 and the Scottish/American pattern. But the conflict, if such it can be called, was then between the rites of different countries when distances were great and communications poor. In the first half of the twentieth century the issue arose anew as to whether the patristic East (principle (b) above) should prevail, with its distinctive epiclesis or whether the Roman rite (principle (e) above) should by its authoritative position impose a doctrine of consecration virtually confined to recitation of the narrative of institution. The conflict was important in the 1920s, as shown, for instance, in the formation of the South African rites of 1924 and 1929, and the 'Deposited Book' rite in the Church of England.[1]

(g) From 1927 onwards the increasing role of communion in the life of the church: the 'parish communion' movement in the Church of England, and the effect on that movement of the liturgical movement of continental Europe. The parish communion movement planted questions about intelligibility, lay participation (and children's communion), and building up the life of the church corporately. It was rarely accompanied by textual revision, but it raised longer-term questions. Communion became the main (indeed the only) service of Sundays in many Anglican parishes.

(h) From 1945 onwards there was a new landmark in *The Shape of the Liturgy*: Gregory Dix was in favour of a return to his understanding of the practice of the

---

[1] See for instance R. C. D. Jasper (ed.) *W. H. Frere: his Correspondence on Liturgical Subjects* (Alcuin Club), and P. B. Hinchcliff, *The South African Liturgy* (OUP, Capetown, 1959).

patristic period and his work deeply affected the perception of liturgical history, within and beyond the boundaries of the Anglican Churches. In particular, revisionists found high priorities in his concepts of the 'four-action shape', 'offertory theology', 'consecration by thanksgiving', and especially in the idea that 'liturgy is essentially something done, not something said'. In addition, he insisted that the Reformation was a real controversy about real issues, and that the Anglican world ought, by its history, its orientation, and the sheer claims of truth, to be found at the catholic end of that controversy. His appeal to the primitive was so compelling, that for many it seemed to provide a way to 'get behind' the controversies of the sixteenth century. Many evangelicals, however, found this an unsatisfactory solution, arguing that it was not possible to avoid the issues of the Reformation merely through an appeal to what preceded it.

(j) The Issues of the 1950s. In this period both Dix and the Parish Communion had a profound, if complex, effect on the liturgical life of the church. Some of the strands of change in this period are as follows:

(i) There were textual changes in seminal form beginning in the Church in South India—the congregational Peace, the restoration (from the Liturgy of St. James, used by Indian Syrian Christians) of the acclamations, and even experiments with offertory prayers.

(ii) There was a revival of interest in architecture and the setting of the liturgy—westwards position for the president, bringing communion tables out from the east wall of the sanctuary, and sometimes placing them closer to the people.[1] The post-war period saw a boom in church building all over Europe. New church buildings sometimes followed a single-room pattern, expressing many of the principles given above—concern with the centrality of the eucharist, the practice of the primitive church, and the importance of lay participation.

(iii) By the end of the 1950s there was considerable desire in many Provinces for textual revision, and the 1958 Lambeth Conference of course gave encouragement to that. There were, however, many who were suspicious of such change, not only out of cultural conservatism, but also through an apprehension that in all the places where serious revision of the eucharist had taken place (e.g. in South Africa, Central Africa, Japan and the West Indies), it had tended towards changes of an anglo-catholic character.

(k) The issues of the 1960s. Many textual revisions have their source in this decade, especially those that followed Dix' hypotheses. The textual revisions of the Roman Church focussed on the Hippolytan model. This model has received several revisions in the 1980s and 1990s, but the Hippolytan model remains as a dominant principle.

---

[1] The practice of placing communion tables away from the East wall and close to the people was anticipated and to some degree achieved by Cranmer and Ridley, who were ridiculed by the Marian counter-reformers for celebrating the sacrament 'on an oyster board'. The practice saw its final reversal in the Ecclesiologist movement's successful indoctrination of the church into their view of the medieval period. See Cranmer's visitation articles.

(l) The issues of the 1970s. In this decade a totally new set of principles arise, possibly (though here I am very tentative) subsumed under the general canon of 'pastoral concerns'. A range of choice of eucharistic prayers begins to be seen as desirable. Anglican revisers may have been following the lead of the Roman revisions coming out of the second Vatican Council in this regard. Also during this time, principally through the influence of the charismatic movement, there was a call for informal eucharists and for 'agapes'. There was much greater recognition that a large part of the eucharistic rite, as it is actually celebrated, need not be prescribed anyway (obviously hymnody and preaching evaded central control—but it was not usually advertised or noticed, even by those who were arranging eucharists). Thus open-weave liturgy started to appear, encouraging local creativity and use of laypersons in all sorts of roles. There was also the first serious and sustained challenge to confirmation as the gateway to communicant standing, an issue not directly in view in textual revision, except in so far as it bears upon the provision of eucharists that are written for the pastoral needs of children, a concept in the writing of eucharistic prayers which affected the Church of Rome in the 1970s, and has entered into Anglican discussion ten to fifteen years later.[1]

(m) The issues of the 1980s. The last few years have seen a new rash of creativity. One has only to inspect the New Zealand Book (1989) to catch a glimpse of this, but it is true elsewhere also. A wholly new principle (and yet one with Reformation roots) has emerged in the quest for 'inculturation', a process leading to far greater liberties with 'the Anglican tradition' than almost anything we have seen in four hundred years. We have also seen experiments in writing eucharistic prayers based on themes, and the provision of an almost inexhaustible range of greetings, intercessions, and acclamations. There are new discussions about communion from the reserved sacrament and the meaning of lay presidency.

(n) The Issues of the 1990s. Here I speak as a man in the middle of a cloud pretending to give an overview of it. This is a 'Decade of Evangelism', and there are many who are asking how the eucharist and other meetings of the people of God can equip them for their mission.

These principles are the major part of my contribution. I emphasize again that they are not simply part of history—once they come into play, they stay around. They may become weaker, some may even on occasions be renounced; but in genral they survive and exercise some force upon our work of liturgical work today. The task of a discriminating critic is to assess how far along each principle can take us, whilst doing justice to all others which may properly claim our loyalty.

---

[1] The textual issue is whether the 'pastoral needs' in the rite include the needs of non-communicants; or does a eucharistic prayer for use when (non-communicating) children are present *have* to pray for fruitful *reception?*

SOME FINAL QUESTIONS

Looking into the future, we find a miscellaneous set of questions, some of which may become competing principles and some of which may simply go away. But I list them as part of our task of addressing the future.

(a) Suppose we start with the laity, and both see worship as a function of the whole congregation, and see the central place of the church's pattern of meeting as a place for building each other up, what then follows for the eucharist? What 'roles' should laypeople fulfil? How can they make contemporary contributions to the agenda within worship? Indeed, how can the laity be most naturally their own true selves, and express themselves as such within the Liturgy? And what does facilitating all that involve for the leadership?

(b) How can we best keep the peace and the law of the church?

(c) How can we best observe the mean between all the extremes?

(d) Does our eucharistic rite have doctrinal standing? Anglicans have always taken liturgical forms to be an important part of the doctrinal stance of a church—do we have that in view? If so, is that a helpful principle, or not?

(e) There are then inculturation questions; these questions are both liturgical and theological, and were dealt with in an initial way at IALC-3 in 1989.[1] The question is initially one of how to belong to one's culture, and secondarily, a question of the problem of how culture-specific celebration may both attract and repel for the wrong reasons. There are also unresolved issues in the field of multi-cultural celebration—if Seythian, barbarian and Greek are one in Christ, in whose culture are they to worship *together*?

---

[1] David R. Holeton, ed., *Liturgical Inculturation in the Anglican Communion*, (Alcuin/ GROW Joint Liturgical Study 15, Grove Books, Bramcote, 1990).

3. Issues around Ministry and The Eucharist

by Paul Bradshaw and John Gibaut

The issues around ministry and the eucharist are twofold: who may minister and who may preside?

Within the eucharistic assembly varieties of ministries are exercised by different individuals. A contrast may be made between ministries exercised on behalf of the whole body (e.g., the presentation of eucharistic elements and the gathering of alms and oblations) and those that arise from the particular gifts that individuals have received (e.g., singing, reading, welcoming). While the former may—and should—be exercised by any of the baptized, the latter needs to be tested and recognized by the community (e.g., not every baptized Christian should play the organ!).

An important association exists between liturgical ministry and Christian life and witness. For instance, it is anomalous when those designated to read at the eucharist are present in the eucharistic assembly only when appointed to fulfil this liturgical function, or when they live in ways that are a denial of the scriptures they read.

A welcome development in the life of the Anglican Communion is the recovery of the diaconate as a distinctive ministry within the life of the church. There are, however, potential problems raised by the question of the restoration of the diaconate which call for consideration. First, as in the case of the other liturgical ministries, it is undesirable for deacons to be mere liturgical functionaries who do not fulfil their *diakonia* in a broader context in and for the church. Second, it is noted that there is a tendency to assign to a deacon in the eucharist all the liturgical functions ever fulfilled by deacons in the course of the history of Christian liturgy. Such a penchant can impede the liturgical ministries of others.

Related to the correlation between liturgical ministry and a broader sense of ministry in and for the church is the issue of eucharistic presidency. All Christian communities require pastoral leadership for the fulness of their life and witness in the world, and as a sign of their communion within the Church universal. In the Anglican tradition, this ministry is exercised by bishops and presbyters. According to ancient principle, it is because these ministers preside over the community that they preside over its eucharistic worship—and not the other way around.

Eucharistic presidency includes gathering and dismissing the community; overseeing the ministry of the word, the intercessions, and the peace; leading the community in its eucharistic action by taking and giving thanks over bread and wine, and by participating in the distribution of holy communion. It is noted, however, that overseeing the liturgy does not mean performing every liturgical ministry. For instance, overseeing the ministry of the word does not have to entail reading or preaching; others may lead the prayers of the people and assist the presider by preparing the eucharistic gifts and by sharing in the fraction and distribution of holy communion.

In those communities where pastoral leadership is not the ministry of one person alone but is shared by a college of presbyters, or by a bishop with his or her presbyters, it is appropriate for this form of leadership to be expressed liturgically. Collegiality can be expressed by the other presbyters being visually associated with the presider through the entire eucharistic celebration, but not by their participation in presidential words or gestures.

A concern voiced by some in the Anglican Communion involves the dilemma of a local community that lacks a presbyter. What happens to the eucharistic life of such communities? There are three possible options regarding the eucharist and this situation.

First, there is distribution of holy communion from the reserved sacrament by a deacon or lay person. While this practice occurs in some parts of the Anglican Communion, it is argued that, in effect, it separates pastoral leadership from liturgical leadership. If it is argued that if those who distribute holy communion are people who already exercise pastoral leadership in the community, why are they not ordained as presbyters for that community? Besides, historically, communion from the reserved sacrament is intended for the pastoral care of those unable to be present at the eucharistic assembly, not the eucharistic assembly itself.

Second, it is proposed that eucharistic celebration be presided over by a deacon or a lay person. The argument about the separation of pastoral and liturgical leadership advanced above also applies to this situation. Should a bishop decide to authorize a deacon or lay person to act as a diaconal or lay presider of a eucharistic community, such persons would be exercising presbyteral functions and therefore should be ordained as presbyters.

The third option for communities that lack a presbyter for a short time is to forgo eucharistic worship altogether. Where, however, the absence is extended, the solution is for presbyters to be raised up for those communities.

4. Eucharistic Consecration, The Role of the Institution Narrative in the Eucharistic Prayer, and Supplementary Consecration

by William Crockett

Research in the history of the eucharistic prayer in recent years calls for a rethinking of our inherited notions of eucharistic consecration, the role of the institution narrative in the eucharistic prayer, and the idea of supplementary consecration. Thomas Talley's essay in this volume has made this clear.

The tradition of the eucharistic prayer evidently derives from Jewish models, particularly Jewish table prayers of blessing and thanksgiving (*berakoth*), and characteristically the thanksgiving said over the cup at the end of the meal, the *birkat ha-mazon*.[1] Precise derivation, however, cannot be established from the limited evidence. The earliest structure of the eucharistic prayer is thanksgiving (for creation and/or redemption) followed by supplication (with an eschatological note). This basic structure developed by way of expansion, but in different ways. In one tradition (notably *The Apostolic Tradition* of Hippolytus[2]) the thanksgiving section was expanded by the addition of an institution narrative/anamnesis unit and the supplicatory section became an epiclesis of the Spirit. In other traditions (Addai and Mari[3], the Strasbourg papyrus[4], the Jerusalem tradition[5]) an institution narrative/anamnesis unit is lacking. By the end of the fourth century the former pattern predominated in the east.

Thomas Talley has observed that the thanksgiving section in all these prayers has a kerygmatic function. The shift from the first to the second section of the prayer is from thanksgiving/proclamation to supplication. The role of the institution narrative/anamnesis unit, where it was added, is likewise proclamatory.[6] It maintains the Christological foundation of the prayer.[7] The

---

[1] R. C. D. Jasper and G. J. Cuming, *Prayers of the eucharist: early and reformed*, 3d ed., rev. and enl. (Pueblo Publishing Co., New York, 1987), 7-12, hereafter cited as *PEER*.

[2] *PEER*, 31-38.

[3] *PEER*, 39-44.

[4] *PEER, 52-54.* See G. J. Cuming, 'The Anaphora of St. Mark: A Study in Development,' in *Le Muséon, 95 (1982): 115-29.*

[5] *PEER*, 82-87. See John Fenwick, *Fourth Century Anaphoral Construction Techniques*, Grove Liturgical Study No. 45 (Grove Books, Bramcote, Notts., 1986), 13-15.

[6] Thomas J. Talley's essay in this volume deals with this subject. I am greatly indebted to Professor Talley for his work in this area.

[7] See Terrance W. Klein, 'Institution Narratives at the Crossroads' in *Worship*, 67 (1993): 407-18.

fundamental structure of the eucharistic prayer in the east, therefore, through all the variety in its development, is thanksgiving/supplication.[1]

In the west, in the developed Roman canon, the note of thanksgiving is retained only in the preface, thus obscuring the earlier structure of the eucharistic prayer. In the post-sanctus the note of praise and thanksgiving is subsumed under the note of supplication and the institution narrative is consequently interpreted in a supplicatory context rather than in the context of thanksgiving/proclamation.[2] It is a short step from Ambrose[3] onwards to interpret the institution narrative as the 'moment' of consecration when the elements are transformed. This paves the way for the medieval development in which the role of the institution narrative becomes a formula of consecration.[4] The new eucharistic prayers in the Roman Sacramentary represent an attempt to restore the primitive structure of the eucharistic prayer. This structure is obscured, however, by the insertion of a consecratory epiclesis before the institution narrative, which reinforces the medieval interpretation of the role of the institution narrative as a formula of consecration.[5]

Luther and Calvin restored the proclamatory function of the institution narrative, but at the cost of isolating it from the prayer of thanksgiving, either by way of dropping the canon altogether (Luther[6]) or by placing it outside the eucharistic prayer (Calvin[7]). Cranmer retains the eucharistic prayer, with the institution narrative as an integral part, but the thanksgiving structure of the prayer is lost in the 1552 rite.[8] It is an open question whether the institution narrative has a consecratory role for Cranmer at all.[9] Richard Buxton has argued that the predominant theory of consecration held by Anglicans (and Puritans) in the seventeenth century is that the elements are consecrated by the institution narrative in the context of the eucharistic prayer.[10] Consecration, however, is no longer understood as a transformation of the elements, but as their setting apart from a 'common' to a 'holy' use, i.e. for the purpose of communion.

Supplementary consecration has no parallel in liturgical traditions outside Anglicanism. Cranmer himself made no provision for it in the Prayer Books of 1549 and 1552 (although provision for supplementary consecration of the

---

[1] Talley, 2-3.
[2] PEER, 159-66. Talley, 3-5.
[3] PEER, 143-46.
[4] See John H. McKenna, *Eucharist and Holy Spirit*, Alcuin Club Collections No. 57 (Mayhew-McCrimmon, Great Wakering, 1975), 72-73.
[5] Talley, 6.
[6] PEER, 189-99. See Bryan Spinks, *Luther's Liturgical Criteria and his Reform of the Canon of the Mass* (Grove Liturgical Study No. 30, Grove Books, Bramcote, Notts., 1982).
[7] PEER, 213-18.
[8] PEER, 232-49.
[9] See Colin Buchanan, *What did Cranmer think he was doing?* (Grove Liturgical Study No. 7, Grove Books, Bramcote, Notts., 1976). The title 'Prayer of Consecration' appears first in the 1662 rite.
[10] Richard F. Buxton, *Eucharist and Institution Narrative*, Alcuin Club Collections No. 58 (Mayhew-McCrimmon, Great Wakering, 1976), 130-32.

chalice had been made in the 1548 Order of Communion). The first subsequent provision for supplementary consecration (by recitation of the institution narrative) is found in Canon 21 of the Canons of 1604. This provision was subsequently enshrined in the 1662 BCP. The motive for introducing supplementary consecration in Anglicanism appears to stem from the close link between consecration and communion in Anglican eucharistic theology. A problem is created, therefore, when there are insufficient consecrated elements for all communicants. The difficulty with the idea of supplementary consecration, however, is that it assumes a moment of consecration in the rite which can be repeated. If, on the other hand, the entire eucharistic action is viewed as a unity, we may want to ask ourselves whether a fresh supply of bread and/or wine may be integrated into the rite without the use of a formula of consecration.[1]

If this historical/theological analysis is correct, the primary context in which the role of the institution narrative ought to be interpreted is the context of thanksgiving/proclamation in the eucharistic prayer. From this perspective, the role of the institution narrative is proclamatory. It maintains the Christological foundation of the prayer. It is not a formula of consecration. This has important implications for future Anglican eucharistic revisions. For example, from this perspective, we ought to ask ourselves whether the provision of an epiclesis before the institution narrative does not obscure the basic thanksgiving/supplication structure of the eucharistic prayer. Likewise, we ought to ask ourselves whether the practice of supplementary consecration by formula does not obscure the unity of the eucharistic action by inserting a moment of consecration into the rite.

---

[1] For a full discussion of the history and practice of supplementary consecration in Anglicanism see Buxton, especially pp.215-229.

5. Structure of the Eucharist— Some Discussion Issues

by Ronald Dowling

Before looking at some of the issues involved in eucharistic structure, it is important to acknowledge that structure is more than the arrangement of textual elements, it is multidimensional, and involves movement, music, symbol, and many other elements.

Although we must acknowledge the complex nature of the eucharist as a whole, it is widely accepted that the basic structure of the eucharist has two main elements, those aspects of the liturgy focussing on the 'word' and those focussing on the 'table'.

There are issues around the 'word' section involving the ordered reading of the Scriptures. These include the many questions about lectionaries and the rationales that inform any particular lectionary. Currently under wide consideration is the Revised Common Lectionary.

The prayers of the people have traditionally followed the proclamation of the Word, but part of our tradition (as Thomas Talley's paper in this volume illustrates) has seen these included in the Great Thanksgiving (eucharistic prayer). Perhaps this balance might be reconsidered.

The history of the eucharistic prayer is rich and complex. It is generally acknowledged that the pursuit of a single Anglican eucharistic prayer is no longer a feasible goal. In many provinces, a variety of eucharistic prayers are approved for use. A frequent apology for this has been to suggest that the general tendancy is to interpret this as a way of expressing the fullness of Anglican eucharistic theology and practice. How wide these parameters might be is another question. Some suggest that there should be a separate blessing over the bread and the cup, and others offer the possibility of reversing the order of word and table. Whilst these views are not widely held, further discussion is needed.[1]

These basic elements are framed by the opening and closing rites. Whilst there are many individual elements in each of these sections, in actual practice they are often heavily overburdened.

The whole matter of penitence and reconciliation within the eucharist is another issue that needs to be addressed. Apart from the formal confession and absolution there are many other penitential and reconciling elements within the eucharist. In pastoral practice these are often overlooked. There is much debate about whether there should be a formal confession and absolution at every eucharist, and this issue requires examination.

---

[1] For an example of separate blessings see 'Experimental Sunday Services 1993', Diocese of Sydney (Australia).

The recitation of the creed at the eucharist is also a matter requiring recon-sideration. Given that many of the newer versions of the Great Thanksgiving give a fuller confession of faith than the previously approved prayers, we need to ask how necessary it is to recite a creed at every celebration.

The centrality of receiving Communion has sometimes been obscured by other actions such as anointing or laying on of hands occurring at the same, or nearly the same time. Such practices need to be questioned.

Whatever answers are offered to these questions, there will always be a need to adapt structures to their local and immediate context and this will always involve careful planning of the texts themselves as well as the ministers and the com-munity in each local context.

6. Issues Regarding Anglicans, Ecumenism and The Eucharist

By John Gibaut

Perhaps the two most important issues pertaining to the eucharist and ecumenism for Anglicans are the questions of where Anglicans may receive the eucharist and who may receive the eucharist in Anglican churches.

Anglicans may receive the sacrament in all churches of the Anglican Communion and those churches with whom they are in full communion (e.g. certain united churches, and some Old Catholic Churches). Anglicans may also receive in churches where there exist agreements of eucharistic sharing (e.g. Anglican-Lutheran agreements in some parts of the world).

Beyond these situations Anglicans, under certain circumstances may receive the sacrament where they are welcome to do so.[1] Many Reformed and Lutheran churches will happily welcome Anglicans to the eucharist, some will not. For many churches eucharistic communion is the goal of ecumenical endeavour, not its means. Accordingly, Anglicans will not normally receive the sacrament in Roman or Eastern-rite catholic churches, nor in Orthodox churches. In circumstances of pastoral necessity, Christians unable to receive the sacraments in their own communities may request the sacramental ministry of a Roman Catholic minister; this situation could well include Anglicans.[2]

While a certain anguish is frequently felt as a result of the lack of intercommunion, good ecumenical relations are furthered when the eucharistic disciplines of our sister churches are both understood and respected. Moreover, eucharistic

---

[1] Cf. Resolution 48, Lambeth Conference, 1988: 'The Conference recommends that, while it is the general practice of the Church that Anglican communicants receive the Holy Communion at the hands of ordained ministers of their own Church, or of Churches in communion therewith, nevertheless, under the general direction of the bishop, to meet special pastoral need, such communicants be free to attend the Eucharist in other Churches holding the apostolic faith as contained in the Scripture and summarized in the Apostles' and Nicene Creeds, and as conscience dictates to receive the sacrament, when they know they are welcome to do so.' (In Roger Coleman, (ed.) *Resolutions of the Twelve Lambeth Conferences, 1887-1988*, (Anglican Book Centre, Toronto, 1992) p.166).

[2] Cf. Canon 844- §4: 'If the danger of death is present or other grave necessity, in the judgement of the diocesan bishop or the conferences of bishops, Catholic ministers may licitly administer these sacraments [i.e. Eucharist, penance, anointing of the sick] to other Christians who do not have full communion with the Catholic Church, who cannot approach a minister of their own community and on their own ask for it, provided they manifest Catholic faith in these sacraments and are properly disposed.' (*Code of Canon Law*, (Canon Law Society of America, Washington, 1984), p.321).

participation is not limited to the reception of holy communion. In situations where Anglicans are not invited to receive holy communion, they may hear the word of God and offer the priestly ministry of intercession for the church and for the world with their Christian sisters and brothers. Such participation is a sign of the real, though not yet fully restored, communion of the church.

Following the Lambeth Conference of 1968, many churches of the Anglican Communion effectively adopted the stance of 'open communion' with respect to the members of other churches with whom no formal agreements of eucharistic sharing exist.[1] The motivation behind this shift is clearly ecumenical—Anglicans understand eucharistic sharing as a means rather than a goal of Christian unity. The theological basis for this shift is the perception of a degree of Christian unity based on a common baptismal unity.

One may question whether 'open communion' has helped or hindered the cause of Christian unity. The spirit of the ecumenical movement has waned: Christians are no longer scandalized by disunity to the extent they once were when they could not receive holy communion together. Once made, however, 'open communion' is impossible to withdraw without considerable ecumenical damage. 'Open Communion' is a measure of sacramental outreach to individual members of other churches. The churches of the Anglican Communion ought to consider a further step in extending the invitation of eucharistic hospitality to the other churches themselves.[2]

A new, and more serious issue is the explicit invitation—offered either orally or in parish bulletins—to those of other faith traditions to receive the eucharist in Anglican churches. The motivation here seems to be goodwill and hospitality. Such instances do serious damage to the link between baptism and admission to the eucharist, consistently made by the Anglican Liturgical Consultations. Also undermined is the sense of baptismal unity which has been the foundation for 'open communion' with members of other churches. It may well be that those who argue for an integral link between baptism and eucharist will find themselves in an odd middle ground between those who insist on confirmation prior to communion on the one hand and those who advocate the communion of the unbaptized on the other.

---

[1] Resolution 45: 'The Conference recommends that, in order to meet special pastoral needs of God's people, under the direction of the bishop, Christians duly baptised in the name of the Holy Trinity and qualified to receive Holy Communion in their own churches may be welcomed at the Lord's Table in the Anglican Communion.' (Coleman, *Resolutions*, p.166).

[2] This position is well articulated by Methodist ecumenist Geoffrey Wainwright: 'While the official admission of individuals in pastoral emergencies is charitable, while the ultimate sovereignty of the Lord over his sacraments must be maintained, and while the flouting of institutional discipline may bring local and temporary relief, yet the question of ecclesial relations cannot be evaded. That is why we are driven back to the possibility of, and need for communion agreements between the churches.' (Geoffrey Wainwright, 'Intercommunion' in Nicolas Lossky, *et al*, (eds.) *Dictionary of the Ecumenical Movement*, (WCC Publications, Geneva, 1991), pp.519-520).

7. Preserving Unity at Large Celebrations of The Eucharist[1]

by Paul Gibson and Clayton Morris

At the 1991 General Convention of the Episcopal Church (U.S.A.) the eucharistic celebrations were held in a massive convention centre space with a large, central platform. On the platform were seats for the presider, deacons, and readers, and a long altar of imposing dimensions. The congregation was seated at three hundred round tables for ten.

On each of the three hundred tables was a chalice and paten, together with bread and wine sufficient for those at the table. The instructions for each celebration asked that each table should identify a bishop or priest who—remaining at the table—would join the celebrant in consecrating the gifts, in breaking the bread, and in the distribution.

This plan for eucharistic celebration has received considerable criticism, although it has also been cited as a model for other celebrations in similar circumstances.

Eucharistic celebrations which gather huge crowds of people for a liturgy originally designed for a dozen close friends are bound to be difficult. There is simply no way to replicate the ambience of the dining room in a space designed to seat hundreds or even thousands of people. The issue demands exploration. The solution to the problem of communicating thousands of participants at the General Convention was the multiplication of presiders. There may be other solutions which better reflect the church's desire to offer a gospel which affirms the tension of unity and diversity without losing sight of inclusivity.

The eucharist cannot be done alone; it always symbolizes the unity of the immediate community and the whole church. When Paul upbraided the Christians at Corinth for the shortcomings of their eucharistic celebrations (1 Cor. 11), he did so on the grounds that they failed to discern a principle he had already identified, *'Because* there is one bread, we who are many are one body.' (1 Cor. 10.17) Christians remember Jesus in prayer and gesture so that they may be one, one in him, one in one another, and one with the whole realm of nature whose redemption he has inaugurated.

Recent attempts to adapt a rite originally designed for twelve people in an upstairs room for use when hundreds or thousands are present have been based on notions which are relatively new in their current forms. One is that bishops or presbyters other than the presider may be associated with the presider as though they themselves were presiding. This is commonly called 'concelebration', although it should not be confused with the practice of presbyters standing with

---

[1] Adapted from Paul Gibson and Clayton Morris, 'Celebrating the eucharist at large events,' in *Open*, Vol. 39, No. 2, (Summer 1993), p.1.

the presider as a college. Concelebration in its modern form is a laudable attempt by the Roman Catholic Church to replace the practice of private masses with a more corporate expression of priestly identity. This problem was faced by Anglicans in the sixteenth century when it was decided that there should normally be one celebration of the eucharist in each church each Sunday and that priests other than the presider should receive communion with the presider. Anglicans do not belong to a tradition in which the priest was obliged to say a private mass every day, or even every Sunday. The reconciliation of this practice with a focus on the single corporate offering at the eucharist is therefore not a central concern to Anglicans, and the importation of a practice which was meant to do this is unnecessary and confusing.

A second notion is that the proximity of the presider to the bread and wine of the eucharist is a relative matter and may be stretched and stretched until the presider may be out of reach of the elements, which may themselves even be in another room. We may ask if the style of such liturgies adequately reflects the role of the presider as the servant of the people as they open themselves to the unity Christ gives?

There should be one presider whose function is to give unity to the celebration. All baptized Christians at a eucharist are concelebrants, but it is the role of the presider to provide a unified focus in the service of supportive leadership. The people must be fed from bread and wine over which the presider has visibly given thanks. There should be one supply of bread and wine, which should look and taste like bread and wine. Arranging for the distribution of the bread and wine from a central holy table to many points of communion is a diaconal task and is as easily solved by careful liturgical planning as by the multiplication of consecrations or locations of consecration. The standard of liturgy is based on the local congregation; larger gatherings are extraordinary and should not provide models which would be inappropriate if transferred to the context of the local 'family'. A grasp of the roles of bishops, presbyters, deacons, and baptized persons is essential to an understanding of the place of practical detail in planning celebrations for very large congregations. The task is to adapt the liturgy for special circumstances in a way which does not denigrate the full baptismal ministry of each member of the body of Christ.

8. Penance and The Eucharist

by David Holeton

One of the more conspicuous differences between the historic prayer books and more recent eucharistic rites lies in the treatment of penitence and reconciliation. The fifteenth and sixteenth centuries were an age obsessed with guilt. The sacrament most frequently received by the faithful was penance and not the eucharist. Society as a whole was pervaded by a sense of guilt. The liturgies produced by the reformers were well inculturated in that they reflected this obsession with sin and guilt. At the same time, the didactic nature of the age valued words above sign or symbolic acts. Contemporary liturgical revisions are challenging some of those decisions for reasons that are both theological and cultural.

There is no celebration of the eucharist without acts of penitence and reconciliation. These acts are, however, more diverse than is often acknowledged. The fundamental act of reconciliation is the eucharistic action itself. In the New Testament itself the cup of salvation is the 'blood of the covenant which is poured out for many for the remission of sins.' (Mt. 26.28).

The exchange of the peace, dramatizing as it does the Matthean injunction (5.23-24) 'So when you are offering your gift at the altar, if you remember that your brother or sister has something against you, leave your gift there before the altar and go; first be reconciled to your brother or sister, and then come and offer your gift, has restored another dimension of reconciliation to the eucharist. Reconciliation is not just of the sinner with God but reconciliation with God and one another in Christ through the community of grace that is the church. 'Those who say "I love God" and hate their brothers or sisters, are liars; for those who do not love a brother or sister whom they have seen, cannot love God whom they have not seen.' (1 Jn. 4.20)

The peace and *fractio panis* are both worded sign-acts which effect reconciliation. If it were possible to ask a Christian in the early church what prayer of confession was in their eucharistic liturgy, the answer would most likely have been 'the Lord's Prayer' with its petition 'Forgive us our sins as we forgive those who sin against us.' Other than that, we have no evidence for prayers of confession in early eucharistic liturgies. When penitential confessions do begin to figure in eucharistic liturgies, they tend to appear just before the moment of communion. Cranmer is faithful to that tradition when, in the first Prayer Book, the General Confession and Prayer of Humble Access appear immediately before communion itself. Cranmer's innovation was when, in 1552, he moved both these elements away from the moment of communion to before the sursum corda and after the sanctus respectively. One effect of this was to give the confession an independent life of its own detached from the act of communion which was its earlier focus.

As we reflect on the reform and renewal of eucharistic rites, it is appropriate that the expression of penance and reconciliation be on the agenda. In an age not obsessed with sin and guilt, is it appropriate for the church to perpetuate the particular concerns of the age of the reformers? What effect should the heightened sense of the corporate nature of sin have on our liturgical reforms? If reconciliation can be understood in terms greater than a prayer of confession and an absolution (peace, *fractio panis*, Lord's Prayer) is it not possible to reserve the use of a confession and absolution to a particular liturgical season (e.g. Lent) or to times when a corporate confession of sin is appropriate in the liturgical community? If, historically, it was the moment just before communion that attracted short expressions of penitence, is that the place where such devotional acts should occur once again? Is the couplet 'Behold the Lamb of God, behold the one who takes away the sin of the world' . . . 'Lord I am not worthy to receive you, speak but the word and I shall be healed.' which seems to be finding its way into Anglican liturgical practice (probably more often unofficially than officially) an appropriate popular penitential expression that should be allowed to find its way into new eucharistic texts?

It is clear from an examination of modern Anglican eucharistic rites that the question of penitence and reconciliation has been on the agenda in every instance. In most revisions this has been marked by a lightening of the heavily penitential character of the traditional Prayer Books. Often this has been greeted with some negative reaction and the revisers are accused of being 'soft on sin'.[1] The majority of regular parishioners, however, have greeted the new treatment of sin positively and find that a less relentless emphasis on sin in the new texts enables them to take the personal and social dimensions of sin more seriously than they have in the past. While the exchange of the peace has been restored in virtually every modern Anglican eucharistic liturgy, there seems to be only a modest amount of work done on its character as an expression of penitence. Very little reflection on the other penitential dimensions of the eucharistic liturgy (*fractio panis*, Lord's Prayer) seems to have taken place. All of these questions need to be on the agenda if the question of penitence and reconciliation in the eucharist is to have the comprehensive discussion it deserves before the next round of revised liturgies begins to appear.

---

[1] This accusation is certainly not new in that the draft of the 1959 Canadian revision of the BCP, a revision which only made cosmetic changes to the sixteenth century text was denounced as containing '. . . questionable, unscriptural and emasculated theology which removes all reference to the pitiable state of mankind, and makes no attempt to translate traditional terms describing the judgment of God.' *Church Times* commentary in Howard H. Clark, *Prayer Book Revision in Canada* (Toronto 1958) p.3.

9. Ceremonial, Ritual Gesture and The Eucharist

by David Holeton and Charles Wallace

It has been noted repeatedly in this collection of essays that the eucharist is more than a printed text—it is an action which involves embodied beings. As such, posture and gesture are expressions of attitude and belief of similar importance to the words we use. This is as true of the posture of the celebrating community as it is of the presiding bishop or priest. The reform of eucharistic rites has implications for both posture and gesture. This phenomenon is hardly new and was certainly a concern of the authors of the first prayer books and a battleground for the generations which followed. The basic inclination of the prayer book reformers of the sixteenth century was to simplify rite and gesture and to abolish the so-called 'dark and dumb ceremonies' which were, by then, vestigial remnants of sign-acts which once 'spoke' their own meaning. At the same time the reformers left much medieval ceremonial (e.g. kneeling for communion) unexamined; this was to become the fuel for much acrimonious debate. Both the reformers and their critics saw the matter as one of theological importance and not as an indifferent matter of ritual 'taste'.

Similar questions face us today. As in the sixteenth century the initiative for change is theological. The strong visceral reaction the changes often elicit perhaps underlines the reality that actions often affect us more than words. A reflection on the strong reaction in many communities to the introduction of the exchange of the peace should make this point. Few changes elicited such negative reaction ('I don't come to church to greet my neighbour.' . . . 'I come to church to be left alone.'), yet few sign-acts are as fundamental to the nature of the eucharistic assembly or as proleptic of what we are called to be.

What are some of the questions that face us as we continue to renew our eucharistic rites? A fundamental one concerns our primary posture for prayer. The reformers left the relatively modern custom of kneeling for the eucharist untouched. Whether this was because it reflected their profoundly penitential eucharistic piety or whether it was one question of popular religion they were unprepared to challenge is unclear. In many parishes around the Communion the more traditional posture of standing has once again become normative. This reflects the reality of the baptismal life of those who have died with Christ and stand risen in him. This is particularly true on the Lord's Day and during the Fifty Days of Easter. Kneeling then has its own penitential character emphasized when it again becomes the posture for prayer on important penitential days (Ash Wednesday and Lent in particular). Similarly, receiving communion standing—and in procession—makes a theological statement about communion as food for the journey that takes us out into the world that is quite a different statement from that made by the more inward-oriented posture of kneeling (often with eyes closed).

When it came to the eucharistic prayer, the reformers were much bolder in reforming ritual gesture. The first prayer books made virtually no provision for the myriad signs of the cross, elevations or osculations that had accompanied the mediaeval *canon missae*. It is naive to think that those who had been priests before the publication of the Order of the Communion in 1548 or the Prayer Book of 1549 all changed their gestures immediately. But when rubrics governing gesture appeared, they were austere in the extreme: the bread was to be broken, the cup and flagon(s) containing the wine touched. As gestures, they were intended to be imitative of what was thought to have happened at the Last Supper. Visibly, however, they could be seen to reinforce particular ideas of a 'moment of consecration'.

Thomas Talley's paper in this collection challenges us to rethink these prayer book gestures. If the *verba* or institution narrative is to be conceived as part of the proclamatory part of the prayer, does not touching, breaking, signing with the cross, genuflecting or bowing towards the elements at this point 'say' quite clearly that the character of the prayer has changed and that the presider is 'doing' something to the elements (presumably consecrating) other than giving thanks over them? Similarly, when the presider extends his/her hands together over the elements during the epiclesis (the traditional sign-act for invoking the Spirit) is he or she not clearly signifying that something is happening at this moment that is not happening elsewhere in the prayer? The unexamined preservation of ritual gesture can undermine everything that this Conference and the Dublin Consultation might try to say about eucharistic prayer.

What then should be the attitude of the presider in the eucharistic prayer? Perhaps just the simple *orans*—hands lifted in prayer. It is this posture that is the common inheritance of all the baptized. It is a gesture of openness and praise, and it could again become the common posture of all 'who are counted worthy to stand in God's presence to serve him' at the eucharistic banquet.

10. The Epiclesis and the Role of the Holy Spirit in the Eucharistic Prayer

by David Kennedy

It is noticeable that Anglican eucharistic rites over the last twenty years give more eloquent expression to the role of the Spirit in the eucharist. Moreover, recent ecumenical statements involving Anglicans in dialogue all affirm that within the eucharistic celebration the elements 'become' Christ's body and blood by the power of the Spirit. In practice, however, contemporary eucharistic prayers reveal diverse approaches to the epiclesis. There is divergence of structure in that some prayers have a preliminary epiclesis before the narrative of institution and in some cases further reference to the Spirit after the anamnesis, while others have a single epiclesis following the anamnesis. There is diversity of content: some prayers include an invocation of the Spirit upon the elements only, some upon the worshippers only, some upon the elements and the worshippers, and some where there is a studied ambiguity. A few recent prayers invoke the Spirit upon the whole eucharistic action.

As Anglicans work towards consensus in this area of eucharistic practice, a number of questions must be raised:

1. In his paper in this volume, Thomas Talley has argued that a single epiclesis in the 'Greek' position after the anamnesis solves the theological problems raised by either a single epiclesis before the institution narrative or a double epiclesis placed before the institution narrative and after the anamnesis. Is this a solution that would commend itself to most Anglican Provinces as they further revise their eucharistic liturgies? In relation to structure, is a single post-anamnesis epiclesis most appropriate, as argued by Thomas Talley in this volume?

2. Would there be better hope of a consensus about the role of the epiclesis if the Spirit was invoked upon the whole eucharistic action, embracing the eucharistic community as well as the elements, thus showing the link between consecration of the elements and the consecration and empowering of the church through reception? Is the epiclesis therefore best understood in a relational sense, linking the elements and worshippers to the whole action of the eucharist and embracing both objective and subjective dynamics? Does such a broad understanding of the role of the Spirit set us free from seeing the epiclesis as a consecratory formula?

3. How do we understand the relationship of the Spirit to material things? There is resistance in some parts of the Communion to an invocation of the Spirit upon the elements. Some fear an epiclesis on the elements presupposes a false dualism between what is 'holy' and what is 'common'. Others fear that rejection of an epiclesis on the elements betrays another dualism—the utter separation of spirit and matter which in the eucharist ought to be reconciled.

What light does Scripture bring to the understanding of material gifts as vehicles of divine blessing? Do verbs such as 'bless', 'sanctify', 'make holy', necessarily imply objective change in the elements or can they be understood as affirming that through the presence and power of the Spirit the elements are vehicles of sacramental grace?

4. How should the presence and reality of the Spirit be expressed in other parts of the rite? If, in the eucharistic prayer, the epiclesis is essentially part of the supplicatory movement and therefore mainly instrumental, what expression should be given to Pentecost and the continuing role of the Spirit in the church in the preface, or first proclamatory part of the eucharistic prayer?

11. Language and The Eucharist

by Gillian Mendham

The desire to make intelligible the liturgies through which we worship God has driven twentieth century liturgical revision, with varied success. One aspect of this revision has involved the transition from traditional to more contemporary forms of language. Some have resisted the updating of language, regretting the loss of its poetic and literary qualities. On the other hand, some who work with less literate populations demand very simple language.

What constitutes intelligible language remains undefined and the subject of debate. No one contests that semantic and grammatical changes have taken place. But how far and to which forms of language should the Church move? We lack an arbiter who will say whose interests have priority. Divergent groups report the experience of linguistic exclusion: many women are unable or unwilling to continue making the effort to reinterpret the word 'men' ('That must include me—the dictionary says so'). Sometimes the young, the differently abled and people of colour respond analogously to images of sight, hearing, light and darkness, mobility and age. The dispossessed are increasingly unwilling to be patient with the white, middle class, male cultural prescription for standard English and the consequent naming of the God who is worshipped and the people who worship.

Liturgy above all involves an address to and encounter with God, and how we name what we experience affects us. Traditionally, instead of drawing on the breadth of the Scriptures, liturgical language has limited itself to a select few metaphors, principally 'Father', 'Lord' and 'Almighty', so much that some would argue that certain ways of naming God are not metaphorical at all but somehow analogical to God's essential nature. For the worshipping church, the theological content of liturgy constitutes a primary teaching resource. What is the effect on people of naming God in ways that have no connexion with who they are? If the only words for God used are masculine, how do women understand themselves in relation to God? If the words we use reflect only God's power and transcendence, are we in danger of losing sight of God's love and involvement with us? Do images of God which reflect how our cultures define femininity somehow change the nature of the Christian revelation? Do such images automatically lead to an understanding of God as an earth-mother or goddess, and what are the implications if they do?

Worship is more than the words we use, but the words we use, because they appear in authorized texts, are slow to change, establish the law of prayer, and thus, the law of belief for the present generation, and, possibly, the generations to come. Because of this, we need to reflect deeply on the language we are using in the eucharistic liturgy, and consider the need and the possibility of reforming it, where helpful or necessary.

12. The Common Cup and Common Loaf

by Ruth A. Meyers

In the celebration of the eucharist, the common cup of wine and common loaf of bread are important symbols of the unity of the body of Christ. Paul reminds the fractious Christian community at Corinth, 'we who are many are one body, for we all partake of the one bread' (1 Cor. 10.17). By sharing the common cup and a common loaf, the unity Christians share with Christ and with one another by virtue of their baptism is made manifest. Restoration of the common cup to the laity, the use of the single loaf, and the elimination of masses at which only the priest communicated were important accomplishments of the Reformation. Wafer bread only began to be used again in the nineteenth century, and only became common in many provinces after the last World War. Consequently, in many, if not most, parts of the Anglican Communion, contemporary eucharistic practice obscures the symbolism of the common cup and common loaf.

In many places, individual wafers are used as a matter of course. This 'bread' which does not look, smell, or taste like the bread used for common meals is a poor substitute for a common loaf that must be broken to be shared. The liturgical movement of the twentieth century, with its emphasis on the body of Christ gathered to celebrate eucharist, has prompted a return to 'real bread' in some parts of our Communion, but individual wafers are still used in many places.

Large celebrations are more problematic: how can we adapt what was originally a meal for a few friends for use by hundreds or thousands of people? In some places, 'preconsecrated' bread and wine are used; elsewhere multiple cups of wine appear on the altar/table; in other circumstances, bishops and presbyters hold vessels of bread and wine (sometimes standing at a great distance from the presider) while the presider recites the eucharistic prayer. All of these solutions obscure the focus on a common cup and common loaf as well as the significance of a single presider who gives unity to the entire celebration.

Particularly vexing are questions of hygiene and the common cup. The spread of AIDS in the late twentieth century has led to fear of contamination from sharing a common cup. This extends to concern about other communicable diseases, for example, forms of hepatitis. Research in this area, however, would indicate that such fears are largely unfounded. Intinction, in some places with a separate 'intinction cup', has been used as a method to avoid transmission of disease. Some Anglican parishes have begun to use individual cups, following the practice of many Protestant denominations. Both of these solutions undermine the symbolism of drinking from a common cup.

Solutions to the problems of large celebrations and responses to anxieties about the transmission of disease need to be carefully evaluated for their impact on the symbolic eucharistic action of sharing a common cup and common loaf. Partaking of one bread and drinking from one cup are central to Anglican tradition, and modifications of this practice should be undertaken only after thorough consideration of the implications of such variations.

13. Communion without a Priest?

by Harold Miller and Phillip Tovey

'We have taught people to hunger for the eucharist and now we are not able to feed them.' This is a description of the position of some of the provinces in the Anglican Communion. Consonant with the desire of the English reformers, communion has become much more frequent, and in many parishes, it has become the weekly norm. This is due both to the evangelical and catholic revivals of the last century, and their missionary activity, and also to the Liturgical Movement in this century, which has stressed the centrality of the eucharist. But what happens if there is no priest? Four possibilities exist:

The first option is the provision of more priests—an obvious and fundamental solution. But what kind of priests? In some places the answer has been the development of 'community priests'. Are there dangers in the de-professionalization of the clergy? Is professionalism a scriptural or historical foundation for a theology of holy orders?

Second, communion could be administered from the reserved sacrament. This has been a growing practice in the Communion in recent years.[1] It has also been controversial, and some provinces have tried to discourage, or even ban it. What does this say about the relationship between priest and people? Is it implicitly 'magical' in its approach to the consecrated elements?

Third, it is possible to hold a non-eucharistic service. Morning Prayer has nourished many Anglicans in their spiritual life. In many parts of the world, these liturgies are led by lay people, sometimes readers or catechists. Are pressures due to clergy shortages directing us back to this type of service, or is this an easy route to avoid issues surrounding the reform of ordination practices?

The fourth option is that lay people could be authorized to preside at the eucharist. This happens in other churches (e.g. Methodist and Reformed churches) without apparently having serious consequences for church order. This option was seriously examined by the Province of the Southern Cone.[2] It is also being considered by the Diocese of Sydney and other Provinces including the Church of England. It would be a serious departure from Anglican tradition, but the issue needs to be carefully examined.[3]

If we are to continue to try to make the eucharist the main Sunday act of worship, then serious study of these various options will be necessary.

[1] D. Smethurst, *Extended Communion: An Experiment in Cumbria* (Grove Worship Series No. 96, Grove Books, Bramcote, 1986); P. Tovey *Communion outside the Eucharist* (Alcuin/GROW Joint Liturgical Study no. 26, Grove Books, Bramcote, 1993).

[2] A. Hargrave, *But Who will Preside?* (Grove Worship Series No. 113, Grove Books, Bramcote, 1990).

[3] Paul Gibson describes the state of Anglican discussions concerning lay presidency in 'The Presidency of the Liturgy' in T. Talley (ed.) *A Kingdom of Priests* (Alcuin/GROW Joint Liturgical Study no. 5, Grove Books, Bramcote, 1988), pp.31-38, and resists such a policy. John Gibaut and Paul Bradshaw's essay in this volume also opposes the concept of lay 'presidency' at the eucharist.

14. The Eucharistic Species and Inculturation

by Juan Quevedo-Bosch

Liturgists have established that the liturgical life of the early church was quite a bit more varied than it was once thought to have been. Although baptism and the 'breaking of the bread' were observed throughout the church, the form and shape of these liturgies varied from place to place and evolved over time.

From the beginning of the history of the church, however, bread and wine were the species used in the eucharist. They were strongly associated with the family act of worship, which contrasted dramatically with the temple cultus with its animal sacrifices and elaborate ceremonies. Jesus founded the rite of the gospel on this tradition of family worship at meals, using the symbols of the Mediterranean culture in which he lived. This started a process of inculturation and cultural insertion that continued in a natural, unsystematic way for twenty centuries.[1]

The use of bread and wine at the eucharist is not only the oldest, but also the most continuously maintained tradition in this process, although the form and amount used belongs to the evolution of the tradition. The process of inculturation and acculturation that continues today should take this fact seriously. The gospel includes both a confrontation with elements of a culture that do not resonate with its message, and an acceptance of elements of culture that do. Critical analysis of both the tradition and the culture has to precede any major changes in Christian practice.[2]

The Nigerian writer, E. E. Usukuwu, comments critically on the exclusive use of wheat bread and wine in the Roman Catholic Communion in Africa. His concerns and suggestions mirror those of many Anglicans. He sees a danger in the lack of a connection between the fruits of the earth, offered or set apart under the symbol of bread in the eucharist, and the significance of 'bread' for many ethnic groups in Africa.[3] There are other voices in the church, who suggest the use of food items with a cultural meaning quite different from bread and wine. Some experimentation along these lines has taken place.

---

[1] Anscar J. Chupungco, *Liturgies of the Future*, (Paulist Press, New York, 1989), pp.25-33.

[2] 'Down to Earth Worship' in *Findings of the Third International Anglican Liturgical Consultation* (Grove Books, Bramcote, 1989) and in D. Holeton (ed.) *Liturgical Inculturation in the Anglican Communion*, (Alcuin/GROW Joint Liturical Study no. 15, Grove Books, Bramcote, 1990).

[3] E. E. Usukuwu, 'African Symbols and Christian Liturgical Celebration', in *Worship*, 62, 2, March 1991, pp.98-112.

There are numerous questions that arise from this particular issue. I will only outline four of them:

1. How can we resolve the tension between the integrity of the gospel and the necessity of its incarnation in cultures that are different from the Mediterranean culture in which the gospel was first incarnated?

2. How can we avoid the main drawback of inculturation, namely diverting the meaning of symbols in directions that are sometimes foreign to their original meaning?

3. How does the use of other food items as the eucharistic species challenge the catholicity of the church, which is already tried by other, perhaps more pressing issues?

4. What is the meaning of bread and wine for a given culture? Are they viable signs of the presence of Christ among the Christians who are members of that culture? How far has the church gone from understanding the gospel to be a part of the culture of the Mediterranean basin?

There are no universally valid answers to these questions, but frontiers should be established. Pastoral concerns should be addressed, cultural integrity should be respected, tradition should be consulted, and the catholicity of the church should be kept.

15. Mission and The Liturgy
Gospel Story and Liturgical Structure
by Charles Sherlock

GOSPEL AND STORY

The gospel of Christ is a story, not an abstract idea. It is a story that demands to be told and re-told. God in Christ is its central character, so that its beginning and end are hidden from us mortals. Yet we do know the hinge around which the plot revolves—the life, death and resurrection of Jesus Christ.

A unique feature of the gospel story is that hearers not only listen to it, but are drawn into it. The Spirit of Christ makes the story of Jesus contemporary. We hear it not only as a mere chronicle of things past, but as a present reality that shapes our lives and our destiny. Jesus Christ is made known to us now in the gospel story, told according to the scriptures. Through this story the Spirit calls us to repent, believe and obey Jesus Christ as Lord. In baptism we come to share his reconciling death and life-giving resurrection, and as children of God and members of Christ's body, are made inheritors of the kingdom of heaven, living now in the light of the future. How does this happen in the liturgy of the church?

LITURGY—TEXT AND SHAPE

Liturgy has often been reduced to shared texts. In today's multi-lingual, multi-cultural, society, this is unhelpful and unrealistic. All Christians continue to receive the text of the scriptures. What this means in practice, however, is not always obvious: how different Romans 13 sounds in Pakistan, China, Britain or Ireland. Liturgical acts such as the confession of sin, the sharing of the peace, or the reception or giving of a blessing take on different significance when experienced in different social and economic contexts.

How then does the gospel story shape the liturgy of the church? I would suggest that the word 'shape' is a key. Common recitation is an ongoing feature of liturgy in every culture. But how and when it takes place, its relation to song and action, let alone the actual words used, are functions of culture. What matters is that the shape of the liturgical celebration of the gospel reflects the story of the gospel. Gregory Dix applied the question of 'shape' to the question of the eucharistic action. He emphasized that the eucharist is something the church 'does' rather than something that the church merely says.

LITURGY, SHAPE AND MISSION

A similar emphasis on the liturgy as a whole can relate liturgy more clearly to mission. This has always been the case, though not always recognised. Liturgies with strongly developed structures sometimes have a clearer exposition of the doctrine of God. Theology is properly doxology, so that the shape of any liturgy does reflect the understanding of God assumed by the community that produced the text. But structure dominated by concepts forms people only intellectually, and individually—and so hinders the conjunction (in community) of thought, action and attitude necessary to mission.

A particular case is the integration of new members. Common texts, even the Lord's Prayer, can take months of repetition before becoming second nature. Brief responses are assimilated more rapidly, but the intended meaning of short reponses is less clear. Some emphasis on learning texts is important, but if it dominates, newcomers are not only put off, but those that remain will be misformed. On the other hand, where a clear, gospel-story-shaped structure holds the liturgy together week by week, both initial access and ongoing formation are furthered.

In sum, since the gospel is a story, liturgy must reflect that story in its structures.

16. The Architectural Setting of The Eucharist

by David H. Smart

The third International Anglican Liturgical Consultation's 'York Statement' asked whether:
'Gothic [architecture] with nave and choir has been over-valued world-wide? Can existing buildings be imaginatively adapted?'[1]

At York, the major issue under consideration was the cultural appropriateness of what was perceived to be the dominant form of Anglican church architecture. The more general question of what could be done to appropriate inherited spaces and to design new ones for contemporary liturgies has not been dealt with by Anglicans on an international level, and there are good reasons why this is so.

The message imparted by the architectural framing of the eucharist is perceived and internalized as profoundly as that of music, ceremony or language. Liturgy, (at least as perceived by Anglican Christians in the latter half of the twentieth century), is not a principle that has informed the practice of church building equally throughout history. Because of this, the demands of inherited rubrics can seem mild compared to those imposed upon us by inherited liturgical spaces. The issues surrounding the renewal of architecture seem more daunting and complex than those surrounding the renewal of texts: they involve not only where the altar is located, but acoustics, the use of lighting, visual art, vesture, and all of the other components that make up the visual and structural setting of the liturgy.

I propose, however, that we try to deal with the following two questions: How does the arrangement of liturgical furniture, either in inherited buildings, or in proposed ones, shape the people of God, and what can be done to ensure that the shaping is truly in the spirit of our liturgies? And secondly, what does this furniture say about who we are, and what our liturgies mean, by its appearance and how we use it?

Furniture needs to be arranged so that its liturgical function is exegeted by its location. The importance of the table is accentuated by its placement close to the people. Congregations have found many ways of expressing this. The importance of a single liturgical presider is acknowledged by Anglican liturgists (as shown by Paul Gibson and Clayton Morris' article in this volume). The location

---

[1] 'The York Statement, Down To Earth Worship', in David R. Holeton, (ed.), *Liturgical Inculturation in the Anglican Communion* (Alcuin/GROW Joint Liturgical Study no. 15, Grove Books, Bramcote, 1990) p.10.

of the presider's chair is therefore of some importance to the arrangement of the furniture. In long, narrow churches the chair is sometimes placed behind the altar. In churches with wider sanctuaries or chancels, or where the table has been placed in the crossing of the nave, it can be placed beside the table. The placement of the choir in the chancel, popularized in the Victorian age, needs to be questioned because it impedes the congregation's visual participation in the liturgy, and it competes visually with the space occupied by the table and the presider. In small churches, the space occupied by the choir actually restricts the space available for the presider and the table to the point where the table seems to be shoved out of the way, up against the apse wall.

The shape and material of the liturgical furniture are also important. The items of furniture required for the eucharist are small in number, but they give spatial and structural expression to actions of great mystery and antiquity. They should, therefore, be constructed of materials which are capable of imparting those messages within the cultural context of the worshipping community. When it comes to materials and design, the temporary and the portable should be avoided because they are not capable of communicating eternal meanings. Holy tables on wheels and folding presider's chairs are some examples of unfortunate use of materials and designs.

This being said, it must be kept in mind that liturgical furniture is meant to show the existential meanings that everyday objects take on in liturgy. The visual association between liturgical objects and the daily life events that the church liturgizes is much more important to the efficacy of liturgy than has sometimes been imagined. Altars which bear no resemblance at all to tables, or presider's chairs which look like fairy-tale thrones fail to make this connexion.

There is a trend in some places to utilize the church and its furniture for non-liturgical functions. Using the space in which the eucharist is celebrated, or the items with which it is celebrated, for common purposes degrades the relationship between the sacred and the everyday that is celebrated in the eucharist. The blessing or setting aside of spaces for sacred purposes has its warrant in both scripture and human nature. It should not be dismissed lightly.

The issues of how to acheive these desirable goals will have to be dealt with on a local and provincial level. The first step should be education. Successful renewal of our liturgical space depends on our willingness to enter into a critical study of our architectural and artistic inheritance and dialogue with the artists, architects, and scholars who can facilitate the necessary changes in either the style of new buildings, or in the arrangement of old ones.

17. Offering and Sacrifice

Kenneth Stevenson and Bryan Spinks

1. THE LEGACY OF ANGLICAN HISTORY

Although the Anglican Church was conceived in a political struggle between the English Tudor monarchy and the Papacy, it was born out of a movement in which certain theological categories and ways of thinking were under critical attack. High on the agenda of this movement was the reform of the unduly strong practice and concept of eucharistic sacrifice as believed and taught in the later Middle Ages at the celebration of the mass. Reformers such as Luther and Calvin conceded that in certain circumstances sacrifice was a legitimate metaphor but they were nonetheless careful to exclude it from their liturgical formulations. This was true of Cranmer and the early Anglican liturgies, but in a carefully nuanced manner.

The English reformers rightly taught that there was only one perfect sacrifice made once for all—that of the cross. But a sacrifice of praise and thanksgiving was offered by the communicants, with their own self-oblation, before communion (in The Book of Common Prayer of 1549) but after it (in 1552 and 1662). Nevertheless, Cranmer did describe the eucharist as a memorial of the death of Christ. Exegetes tell us that even when scripture calls the death of Christ a sacrifice, this is an essentially metaphorical use of the word. If the eucharist is a memorial of the sacrifice, then by extension of the metaphor the rite has been repeatedly described in the history of the Church as in some sense an offering.

Luther and Calvin conceded this. Many later Anglican divines went further and advocated it, and this included those with high sacramental theologies like Lancelot Andrewes, Puritans, like Richard Baxter, as well as the more liberal' traditionalists such as Jeremy Taylor and Simon Patrick. It is not surprising, therefore, that the concept of eucharistic sacrifice filtered back into eucharistic liturgies from 1637 onwards, nor is it insignificant that such a move went hand-in-hand with the slow reintroduction of a full eucharistic prayer. In modern Anglican rites language about eucharist as sacrifice has tended to cluster around two points: the preparation of the bread and wine before the anaphora, and in a variety of expressions in the anamnesis of the eucharistic prayer. The 1958 Lambeth Conference report on the Prayer Book rightly identified the two strands' in Anglicanism regarding sacrifice, both legitimate, but the Lambeth Fathers may have been prematurely optimistic in the belief that these two strands could at that time be united. Subsequent ecumenical discussion, however, has shown that theologians of different traditions can agree on statements about the eucharistic sacrifice (e.g. ARCIC and BEM).

2. THEOLOGICAL CONTEXT

Any metaphorical language in which the Church claims to be doing something towards God (i.e. Godward) has to be understood in the context of Christology, ecclesiology, soteriology, and eschatology. Anglican attempts to do this may be traced back to the two righteousnesses' so eloquently expressed by Richard Hooker, and which are a commonplace in the classical divines:

'We participate in Christ partly by imputation, as when those things which he did and suffered for us are imputed unto us for righteousness; partly by habitual and real infusion, as when grace is inwardly bestowed while we are on earth.' (*Laws of Ecclesiastical Polity*, Book V, 1vi 11.)

The church is born through the waters of baptism into the Name of the Triune God, into the body of Christ. All that we do in his Name is in, with, and through the one obedient and victorious Christ, who is now before the Father in eternity. Eternity is outside space-time, yet all our language is space- and time-bound. Thus, whether we do this in memory or remembrance, or celebrate, or bring before, or plead the sacrifice, re-present, or offer (all of which expressions and ideas are to be found in the classical divines), the eucharistic action is performed by an eschatological community in Christ at a moment when time and eternity become one in the presence of God. In this context, 'we offer this bread and cup' is no more or less legitimate than 'with this bread and this cup we do as our Saviour commanded'. Within that setting, it is not we but Christ who lives in us who is the agent. As Augustine put it memorably centuries before, 'when God crowns our works, it is his own works that he crowns.'

Questions which arise are:

(1) Some find the use of sacrificial imagery helpful and important, whereas others do not. This is our Reformation inheritance. Should all provinces allow for both attitudes, as well as the variations between?

(2) Where sacrificial imagery is used, it is important to recognize that this is an extension of a biblical metaphor for the work of Christ. How can this extended metaphor be prevented from becoming the single principle which dominates the eucharist? If sacrificial language was abolished or reduced, would there be a serious cost to eucharistic piety?

(3) Is it desirable for such imagery to be used in and around the preparation of the bread and wine? Is this utilitarian action already given too much prominence?

(4) If the eucharistic prayer is the proper context for this imagery of sacrifice, is the anamnesis the only place in which it could occur, or are there other positions that are equally legitimate, e.g. offering the sacrifice of praise before the sanctus (as in the Egyptian Liturgy of St. Mark), or pleading the eternal sacrifice before the epiclesis (as in Church of Scotland rites)?

(5) Are there new areas of inculturation where eucharistic language actually needs to extend the sacrificial metaphor in order to find a new and appropriate climate of faith and practice?

Alcuin/GROW Joint Liturgical Studies

All cost £3.95 (US $8) in 1994

1987 TITLES

1. **(LS 49) Daily and Weekly Worship—from Jewish to Christian**
   by Roger Beckwith, Warden of Latimer House, Oxford
2. **(LS 50) The Canons of Hippolytus**
   edited by Paul Bradshaw, Professor of Liturgics, University of Notre Dame
3. **(LS 51) Modern Anglican Ordination Rites**
   edited by Colin Buchanan, then Bishop of Aston
4. **(LS 52) Models of Liturgical Theology**
   by James Empereur, of the Jesuit School of Theology, Berkeley

1988 TITLES

5. **(LS 53) A Kingdom of Priests: Liturgical Formation of the Laity: The Brixen Essays**
   edited by Thomas Talley, Professor of Liturgics, General Theological Seminary, New York.
6. **(LS 54) The Bishop in Liturgy: an Anglican Study**
   edited by Colin Buchanan, then Bishop of Aston
7. **(LS 55) Inculturation: the Eucharist in Africa**
   by Phillip Tovey, research student, previously tutor in liturgy in Uganda
8. **(LS 56) Essays in Early Eastern Initiation**
   edited by Paul Bradshaw, Professor of Liturgics, University of Notre Dame

1989 TITLES

9. **(LS 57) The Liturgy of the Church in Jerusalem** by John Baldovin
10. **(LS 58) Adult Initiation** edited by Donald Withey
11. **(LS 59) 'The Missing Oblation': The Contents of the Early Antiochene Anaphora**
    by John Fenwick
12. **(LS 60) Calvin and Bullinger on the Lord's Supper** by Paul Rorem

1990 TITLES

13-14 **(LS 61) The Liturgical Portions of The Apostolic Constitutions: A Text for Students**
    edited by W. Jardine Grisbrooke (This double-size volume, costs double price (i.e. £7.90 in 1994)).
15. **(LS 62) Liturgical Inculturation in the Anglican Communion**
    edited by David Holeton, Professor of Liturgics, Trinity College, Toronto
16. **(LS 63) Cremation Today and Tomorrow** .
    by Douglas Davies, University of Nottingham

1991 TITLES

17. **(LS64) The Preaching Service—The Glory of the Methodists**
    by Adrian Burdon, Methodist Minister in Rochdale
18. **(LS65) Irenaeus of Lyon on Baptism and Eucharist**
    edited with Introduction, Translation and Commentary by David Power, Washington, D.C.
19. **(LS66) Testamentum Domini**
    edited by Grant Sperry-White, Department of Theology, Notre Dame
20. **(LS67) The Origins of the Roman Rite**
    Edited by Gordon Jeanes, Lecturer in Liturgy, University of Durham

1992 TITLES

21. **The Anglican Eucharist in New Zealand 1814-1989**
    by Bosco Peters, Christchurch, New Zealand
22-23. **Foundations of Christian Music: The Music of Pre-Constantinian Christianity**
    by Edward Foley, Capuchin Franciscan, Chicago (second double-sized volume at £7.90 in 1994))

1993 TITLES

24. **Liturgical Presidency** by Paul James
25. **The Sacramentary of Sarapion of Thmuis: A Text for Students** edited by Ric Lennard-Barrett,
    West Australia
26. **Communion Outside the Eucharist** by Phillip Tovey, Banbury, Oxon.

1994 TITLES

27. **Revising the Eucharist: Groundwork for the Anglican Communion** edited by David Holeton, Dean
    of Trinity College, Toronto
28. **Anglican Liturgical Inculturation in Africa** edited by David Gitari, Bishop of Klrinyaga, Kenya
    (June 1994)
29-30. **On Baptismal Fonts: Ancient and Modern** by Anita Stauffer, Lutheran World Federation, Geneva
    (September, 1994) (Double-sized volume at £7.90)